The Child Development Associate® National Credentialing Program
and
CDA Competency Standards

COUNCIL
for
PROFESSIONAL
RECOGNITION

The Council for Professional Recognition

2460 16th Street, NW Washington, DC 20009-3547

Local: 202-265-9090   Toll Free: 800-424-4310

Visit the Council's Website at **www.cdacouncil.org**.

Infant/Toddler Edition

Sixth Printing, Printed and bound in the United States of America

January 2016

ISBN: 978-0-9889650-1-0

Table of Contents

Introduction...2

Overview 4

Settings for CDA Assessments 6

Infant-Toddler Endorsement Sub-Groups 7

Part 1

Earning the Child Development Associate® (CDA) Credential™

Earning the Child Development Associate®
(CDA) Credential™...8

    Prepare for the CDA Credentialing Process 10

      Any Time Before You Apply 10

        High School Education 10

        Literacy Skills 10

        Setting..10

        Professional Education 10

        The 8 CDA Subject Areas 10

      Within Three Years Before You Apply..12

        Work Experience 12

      Within Six Months Before You Apply 12

        Family Questionnaires 12

        Professional Portfolio 13

          Preparing Your Professional Portfolio 14

          The Resource Collection 14

          The Reflective Statements of Competence 17

          The Professional Philosophy Statement 20

    Apply for the CDA Credentialing Process 21

      Identify a CDA Professional Development Specialist...21

        Finding a Professional Development Specialist 21

        PD Specialist Eligibility Requirements 21

        PD Specialist Conflicts of Interest..22

Secure your director's permission for your CDA Verification Visit™................23

Complete the CDA application................23

Demonstrate Your Competence 25

The CDA Verification Visit™ 25

Scheduling Your CDA Verification Visit™ 25

Rescheduling Your CDA Verification Visit™ 26

Meeting All Requirements 26

Your CDA Verification Visit™ 27

The CDA Exam................28

Scheduling Your CDA Exam 28

Rescheduling Your CDA Exam 29

Preparing for Your CDA Exam 30

Taking Your CDA Exam 30

Earn your CDA Credential 32

Renew Your Credential 32

Earn a Second Credential 33

Language Specializations 34

Part 2

The Child Development Associate® Competency Standards...........38

Competency Standard I................42

Functional Area 1: Safe................43

Functional Area 2: Healthy 46

Functional Area 3: Learning Environment................51

Competency Standard II................59

Functional Area 4: Physical 61

Functional Area 5: Cognitive 64

Functional Area 6: Communication 67

Functional Area 7: Creative 74

Competency Standard III..77

    Functional Area 8: Self...79

    Functional Area 9: Social..84

    Functional Area 10: Guidance...88

Competency Standard IV 93

    Functional Area 11: Families...94

Competency Standard V...101

    Functional Area 12: Program Management 101

Competency Standard VI 104

    Functional Area 13: Professionalism..104

Part 3

Additional Information

Additional Information 107

    Overseas Assessments...108

    ADA Accommodations...108

    Principles for Dual Language Learners 109

    CDA Professional Development Specialist Eligibility Requirements..................116

    The CDA Verification Visit™ Reflective Dialogue 118

    CDA Exam Questions 121

    Glossary of Terms 123

Resources...128

    Application 129

    My CDA Professional Portfolio..133

    Summary of My CDA Education 135

    Family Questionnaire 137

    Spanish Family Questionnaire 139

    Family Questionnaires Summary Sheet 141

    Reflective Dialogue Worksheet 143

    Comprehensive Scoring Instrument .... CSI 1

Introduction

Dr. Calvin E. Moore, Jr.
Deputy Director, Office of Child Care
U.S. Department of Health and Human Services
Earned his CDA in 1992

Dear Colleagues:

We welcome you as you begin your journey to earn your Child Development Associate® (CDA) Credential™!

The CDA is the "best first step" you can take to work effectively with children and their families.   The CDA Competency Standards offer you a roadmap for what you should know and be able to do effectively in any setting – Infant & Toddler, Preschool, Family Child Care or Home Visitor. And, because the CDA is the only national, multi-language credentialing system, the CDA credential is designed to assess your competency in the language of your daily work.

Since 1971, the CDA National Credentialing Program has been the only comprehensive system of its kind in our country.   We are proud that the CDA continues to be the nation's premier credential for early educators. If you move to another state or community, you can be confident knowing that the CDA is the only portable, transferable, valid, competency-based, national credential recognized in all 50 states, territories, the District of Columbia, community colleges and

MaryEllen Fritz
President and CEO, Family Resource Center
Earned her CDA in 2002

Cristy Lopez
Teacher
Earned her CDA in 2012

Sabrena Smith
Director of Training Programs
Earned her CDA in 1990

Aisha Batty
Family Child Care Provider
Earned her CDA in 1993

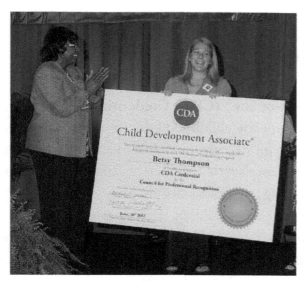

Betsy Thompson
The first high school student to be awarded a CDA (2012)

Brenda Acero
The 300,000ᵗʰ CDA awarded (2012)

the United States military. The CDA is the only credit-bearing national credential that articulates to Associate degrees in most community college systems across the nation. When you earn your CDA, you join a community of over 350,000 early educators!

All of us as at the Council consider our relationship with you to be a sacred trust. We are deeply committed to supporting your professional growth and progress. We look forward to awarding your CDA credential — a distinctive symbol of your accomplishments. We are with you as you take the journey to make an even more powerful difference in the lives of young children!

Sincerely,

Valora Washington

Valora Washington, PhD
CEO
Council for Professional Recognition

Michelle Salcedo
Chief Academic Officer
Earned her CDA in 1994

Jacqueline Whiting
Teacher
Earned her CDA in 1991

Tracy Ehlert
Teacher
Earned her CDA in 2010

Overview

The Child Development Associate® (CDA) Credential™ is the most widely recognized credential in early childhood education (ECE) and is a key stepping stone on the path of career advancement in ECE. The CDA Credential is based on a core set of Competency Standards, which guide early care and learning professionals as they work toward becoming qualified teachers of young children. These professionals have the knowledge of how to put the CDA Competency Standards into practice and the understanding of how the Standards help children move with success from one developmental stage to another.

The Child Development Associate® (CDA) Credential™ is the "best first step" because:

The CDA National Credentialing Program is based on the knowledge of the nation's leading scholars in early care and learning. Utilizing multiple sources of evidence, the Program is the only comprehensive system of its kind that recognizes the essential competencies needed by entry-level and all early childhood professionals. The CDA credentialing process is now a powerful, cohesive professional development experience, infused with meaningful activities that facilitate the reflective practice of working professionals.

The CDA Credential is awarded to early care and learning professionals who work in a variety of settings:

- Infant/Toddler
- Preschool
- Family Child Care
- Home Visitors

Candidates may also apply for Language Specializations:

- **Bilingual Specialization** (for Candidates working in bilingual programs)
- **Monolingual Specialization** (for Candidates working in programs in which a language other than English is spoken) Note: If the language of the Specialization is other than Spanish, the Candidate must contact the Council in order to make special arrangements.

The Child Development Associate® (CDA) National Credentialing Program was established in 1971. The purpose of the program is to enhance the quality of early care and learning by defining, evaluating and recognizing the competence of early care and learning professionals across the country. More than 350,000 child care providers have earned the CDA Credential since 1975, in all 50 states as well as the U.S. territories of Guam, the Virgin Islands and the Commonwealth of Puerto Rico.

The CDA assessment and credentialing of early care and learning professionals has been administered by the Council for Professional Recognition since 1985.

Mission of the Council

The Council for Professional Recognition promotes improved performance and recognition of professionals in the early childhood education of children aged birth to 5 years old.

Vision of the Council

The Council works to ensure that all early care and learning professionals meet the developmental, emotional and educational needs of our nation's (the world's) youngest children.

Identity of the Council

The Council has, for decades, viewed itself as an "assessment" organization whose purpose is to assess the competency of early care and learning professionals and award the CDA credential to all Candidates who meet eligibility requirements and show evidence of meeting the Council's Competency Standards.

Upon the arrival of the Council's current CEO, Valora Washington, in January, 2011, the Council now views itself as having an expanded identity: The Council remains an assessment organization but is also a professional development (PD) organization in which the CDA is the first best step along the PD path. This paradigm shift opens new opportunities for the Council to increase the ways the Mission is met and expand the Vision to include more ways to be of support to young children and the professionals who serve them.

Settings for CDA Assessments

Candidates applying for the CDA Credential must be observed working in a "setting" that meets the following criteria: (NOTE: Candidates may be employed or work on a volunteer basis in the child care setting.)

CENTER BASED SETTING

Preschool Center Based setting is a state-approved child development center where a Candidate can be observed working with a group of at least eight children, all of whom are ages 3 to 5 years. In addition, a center-based program must have: 1) at least 10 children enrolled in the program (not necessarily in the Candidate's group); and (2) at least two caregivers working with the children on a regular basis.

Infant-Toddler Center Based setting is a state-approved child development center where a Candidate can be observed working with a group of at least three children, all of whom are aged birth through 36 months. A Candidate may work/be observed with all sub-groups or with one or two sub-groups*). In addition, a center-based program must have: 1) at least 10 children enrolled in the program (not necessarily in the Candidate's group); and (2) at least two caregivers working with the children on a regular basis.

FAMILY CHILD CARE SETTING

A Family Child Care setting is a family child care home where a Candidate can be observed working with at least two children 5 years old or younger who are not related to the Candidate by blood or marriage. The setting must meet at least the minimum level of applicable state and/or local regulations. Family Child Care settings are also eligible in localities where there is no regulation of family child care.

HOME VISITOR SETTING

A Home Visitor setting is an established program of Home visits (to families with children 5 years old or younger) that supports parents in meeting the needs of their young children, and where Candidates can be observed conducting home visits. In this setting, regular home visits are the primary methods of program delivery.

~ BILINGUAL SETTING
(Required for Candidates who apply for Bilingual Specialization)

A Bilingual setting is a child development program that has specific goals for achieving bilingual development in children; where two languages are consistently used in daily experiences and activities; and where parents are helped to understand the goals and support children's dual language learning.

SPECIAL EDUCATION SETTING

A "Special Education" child development setting — one designed to serve children with moderate to severe special needs — does qualify as an eligible setting for CDA assessment. The CDA Competency Standards address the skills that early childhood educators need for this population of children. The program must meet the other criteria described above for a Preschool, Infant/Toddler, or Family Child Care setting. The chronological ages of the children with special needs also must match the age groups specified for each setting.

NOTE: Drop in programs and before and after school programs are not eligible settings where a Candidate can prove his or her competence around the Competency Standards including all Functional Areas.

Infant-Toddler Endorsement Sub-Groups

In order to demonstrate competence with the complete Infant-Toddler age range, a Candidate applying for a CDA Credential with Infant-Toddler endorsement must:

- Be observed by the CDA Professional Development Specialist working in his/her classroom with any or all of the three Infant-Toddler sub-groups.

Young Infants (Birth - 8 months)	**Mobile Infants** (9 - 17 months)	**Toddlers** (18 - 36 months)

- Complete Professional Portfolio according to Infant-Toddler requirements (see pages 13-20), including those specific resources embedded in the Resource Collection and Reflective Statements of Competence that will allow the Candidate to demonstrate his or her competence with all sub-groups.

 Indicates a required example for Candidates seeking Bilingual Specialization

Professional Portfolio

Observation

Part 1

Earning the Child Development Associate® (CDA) Credential™

1. Prepare for the CDA Credentialing Process
2. Apply for the CDA Credentialing Process
3. Demonstrate Your Competence
4. Earn Your Credential
5. Renew Your Credential

CDA Exam

Reflective Dialogue

Earning the Child Development Associate® (CDA) Credential™

In order to earn and maintain the Child Development Associate® (CDA) Credential™, Candidates must follow the following sequence of steps:

1. Prepare
2. Apply
3. Demonstrate
4. Earn
5. Renew

On the following pages, each of the steps is discussed in detail. You are encouraged to read through the process in its entirety in order to gain a sense of the full credentialing process and its requirements. Once you choose to begin your credentialing process, you may use the Candidate Checklist, found on the inside cover of this book, to track each of your accomplishments as you make your way toward earning the CDA.

Prepare for the CDA Credentialing Process: Candidate Eligibility Requirements

Any Time Before You Apply

High School Education

You must have a valid high school diploma to apply for the Child Development Associate® (CDA) Credential™. A GED or enrollment as a junior or senior in a high school career/technical program in early childhood education are also acceptable.

Literacy Skills

Be able to speak, read and write well enough, in the language required at work, to fulfill the responsibilities of a CDA.

Setting

You must identify a state-approved child development center where you, the Candidate, can be observed working as **lead teacher** with a group of **at least three children**, of any ages between birth to 36 months (a Candidate may work/be observed with all sub-groups or with one or two sub-groups). In addition, a center-based program must have: (1) at least 10 children enrolled in the program (not necessarily in the Candidate's group); and (2) at least two caregivers working with the children on a regular basis.

Professional Education

You must complete 120 clock hours of professional early childhood education, covering the growth and development of children ages birth to 36 months, with no fewer than 10 hours in each of the eight CDA Subject Areas:

The 8 CDA Subject Areas

CDA Subject Area 1. Planning a safe and healthy learning environment

Examples: Safety, first aid, health, nutrition, space planning, materials and equipment, play

CDA Subject Area 2. Advancing children's physical and intellectual development

Examples: Large and small muscle, language and literacy, discovery, art, music, mathematics, social studies, science, technology, and dual language learning

---

1 Prepare

Any Time Before You Apply
- High School Education
- Professional Education -- 120 clock hours, including 10 hours in each of the 8 CDA Subject Areas

Within Three Years of Submitting Application
- Work Experience -- 480 hours of experience working with children ages birth - 36 months

Within Six Months of Submitting Application
- Family Questionnaires
- Professional Portfolio

CDA Subject Area 3: Supporting children's social and emotional development

Examples: Adult modeling, self-esteem, self-regulation, socialization, cultural identity, conflict resolution

CDA Subject Area 4. Building productive relationships with families

Examples: Parent involvement, home visits, conferences, referrals, communication strategies

CDA Subject Area 5. Managing an effective program

Examples: Planning, record keeping, reporting, community services

CDA Subject Area 6. Maintaining a commitment to professionalism

Examples: Advocacy, ethical practices, workforce issues, professional development, goal setting, networking

CDA Subject Area 7. Observing and recording children's behavior

Examples: Tools and strategies for objective observation and assessment of children's behavior and learning to plan curriculum and individualize teaching, developmental delays, intervention strategies, individual education plans

CDA Subject Area 8. Understanding principles of child development and learning

Examples: Typical developmental expectations for children from birth through age 5, individual variation including children with special needs, cultural influences on development, an understanding of early brain development

In order to show proof of your professional education, you must provide transcripts, certificates or letters (originals or copies) in your *Professional Portfolio* (p. 13). This documentation should be preceded by the *Summary of My CDA Education* cover sheet, found at the end of this book on p. 135. At your CDA Verification Visit™, the CDA Professional Development Specialist will review the *Summary* cover sheet and attached documentation.

Acceptable Professional Education

Education may be completed through a wide variety of training organizations, including two and four year colleges, private training organizations, vocational or technical schools, resource and referral agencies and early childhood education programs that sponsor training (such as Head Start or the U.S. Military).

You may accumulate the hours from a single training program or from a combination of programs. Each agency or organization must provide verification of your education in the form of a transcript, certificate or letter on official letterhead. The Council accepts in-service training, but does not accept training obtained at conferences or from individual consultants.

All professional education hours must be awarded by an agency or organization with expertise in early childhood teacher preparation. These hours can be for college credit or for no credit.

Within Three Years Before You Apply

Work Experience

You must have at least 480 hours of experience, within the past three years, working with children ages birth to 36 months in an infant/toddler group setting to apply for the Child Development Associate® (CDA) Credential™. Your experience may be as a paid staff or volunteer.

Within Six Months Before You Apply

Family Questionnaires

Your reflections on family perceptions about your strengths and areas for professional growth are very important in the CDA credentialing process. Each family with a child in your care should be invited to complete a questionnaire.

A *Family Questionnaire* that is reproducible is provided for you at the end of this book on p. 137. Please tear it out and make the appropriate number of copies for distribution among your families. There is also a Spanish *Family Questionnaire* for any Spanish speaking families in your program on p. 139. Note: The *Family Questionnaire* is two-sided – both sides must be copied and distributed to families.

Before copying, fill in the blank spaces in the introduction (your name and the date by which you will need the questionnaires returned to you). Copy and distribute one to each family.

Once you have collected all of the completed questionnaires, please read the responses and reflect on the feedback you have received. Do you notice any patterns or trends among the families' responses about their perceptions of your strengths or areas for professional growth? Remember that there are no "right" or "wrong" conclusions to draw, you must decide for yourself how to best interpret the feedback you have been given. For example, you might notice that 17 out of 20 questionnaires rate you as "very capable" when it comes to promoting health and nutrition (#2). You might conclude that the families, generally, see this as one of your strengths. Similarly, you might notice that 12 out of 20 rate you as "needs improvement" in the area of helping children express themselves creatively through music, art and movement (#7). You might conclude that the families, generally, see this as an area for your continued professional growth.

Conclude the *Family Questionnaire* process by writing any Areas of Strength and/or Areas for Professional Growth you've chosen on the *Family Questionnaire Summary Sheet* found at the end of this book on p. 141. Additionally, write this information in Boxes A and B of the *CDA Verification Visit™ Reflective Dialogue Worksheet*, also found at the end of the book on p. 143. This step is important because your CDA Verification Visit™ will conclude with a reflective dialogue/ discussion with a CDA Professional Development (PD) Specialist in which you will consider this feedback from your families as you set professional goals for yourself.

In addition to the Areas of Strength and/or Areas for Professional Growth you've written on the *Family Questionnaire Summary Sheet*, you must also list the total number of questionnaires distributed and collected. You are required to collect the "majority" (more than half) of the questionnaires you distribute.

Place the *Family Questionnaire Summary Sheet* and completed questionnaires behind Tab B in your Professional Portfolio. Please know that no one but you will read the feedback your families have provided. The PD Specialist will only look at the Summary sheet to verify that you have successfully completed this task.

Professional Portfolio

The *Professional Portfolio* is intended to be a reflective professional development experience for you. You are encouraged to use and add to your Portfolio as you grow throughout your career.

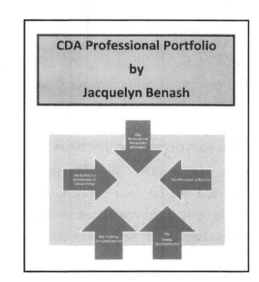

Your Professional Portfolio must include:

a) The *My CDA Professional Portfolio* cover sheet found at the back of this book on p. 133 (this cover sheet provides greater details on the specific order of portfolio components – use it as a checklist as you build your Portfolio to ensure that your completed Portfolio contains all of the required contents)

b) The *Summary of My CDA Education* cover sheet followed by your transcripts, certificates, letters, etc.

c) The *Family Questionnaires* cover sheet followed by your completed family questionnaires

d) Six Reflective Statements of Competence, followed by the related Resource Collection items, as outlined on the *My CDA Professional Portfolio* cover sheet

e) Your Professional Philosophy Statement, which summarizes your professional viewpoint and may take into account new ideas you learned during the building of your Portfolio.

Preparing Your Professional Portfolio

The first step is creating the shell of your Portfolio, into which you will add many items. Your Portfolio may be arranged in any creative way you choose (for example, organized in a three-ring binder, contained inside folders in a file box or even created online). While there are no specific requirements about how it should look, it should be legible, look professional and be manageable in size and portability.

The second step will be to add your *My CDA Professional Portfolio* cover sheet. This portfolio cover sheet will guide you in organizing the contents of your Portfolio using tabbed sections.

You will then add your *Summary of My CDA Education* cover sheet followed by your transcripts, certificates, letters, etc. and your *Family Questionnaires* cover sheet followed by your completed family questionnaires.

Next come the biggest parts of your Portfolio preparation work – the collection of Resources and the writing of your *Reflective Competency Statements*.

The Resource Collection

One of the most valuable components of your Portfolio that you might use in your work moving forward will be your collection of early childhood resources. You may find yourself referring back to these helpful resources in the future as you continue your career. (Note: The numbering of the following list of Resources correlates to each of the Competency Standards.)

Your *Resource Collection* must include the following items:

RC I-1 Your valid and current certificates of completion or cards from a) any **first aid course** and b) an **infant/child (pediatric) CPR course** offered by a nationally-recognized training organization (such as American Red Cross or the American Heart Association). Online training is not acceptable.

RC I-2 Provide one feeding schedule or menu used for each age group (young infants, mobile infants, toddlers). In order to complete your related Reflective Competency Statement on this topic, the feeding schedules and/or menus would ideally be ones that you have participated in serving to and/or designing for children. If this is not possible, or if you work in a program that does not serve meals, you may substitute feeding schedules or menus found on the internet. (More important than the source of the menu will be *Reflective Competency Statement I*, in which you will discuss your opinions about the feeding schedules/menus – what you think are their strengths and/or what you might serve that you think is more appropriate and why.)

RC I-3   A sample of your **weekly plan** that includes goals for children's learning and development, brief descriptions of planned learning experiences, and also accommodations for children with special needs (whether for children you currently serve or may serve in the future). Indicate the age group(s) for which the plan is intended.

RC II   Nine **learning experiences** (activities), written in your own words, including one from each of the following curricular areas:

RC II-1 Science/Sensory

RC II-2 Language and Literacy

RC II-3 Creative Arts

RC II-4 Fine motor (please choose an indoor activity)

RC II-5 Gross motor (please choose an outdoor activity)

RC II-6 Self Concept

RC II-7 Emotional Skills/Regulation

RC II-8 Social Skills

RC II-9 Mathematics

For example, for RC II-1, Science/Sensory, you might write about an experience entitled "Smell Jars" and for RC II-6, Self Concept, you might write about an experience entitled "Self Portraits".

For each activity, indicate the age group (young infants, mobile infants or toddlers) and list the intended goals, materials and process/teaching strategies. For each activity, specify how it is developmentally appropriate for that age group. Of the nine activities, three should be appropriate for young infants, three for mobile infants and three for toddlers.

RC III   A **bibliography** that includes the titles, authors, publishers, copyright dates and short summaries of ten developmentally appropriate children's books *that you have used with young children*. Each book should support a different topic related to children's lives and challenges. Subjects you might consider addressing include:

• Cultural or linguistic group identity

• Gender Identity

• Children with Special Needs

• Separation/Divorce/Remarriage/Family Structures

• Phases of the cycle of life from human reproduction to death

• Other topics that reflect the children and families with whom you work

RC IV   A *Family Resources Guide* that you might choose to share with the families you serve. The Guide should include all of the helpful information you think they might need. At a minimum, you must include the following required items:

       RC IV-1   The name and contact information (phone number, web site, etc.) of a local agency that provides family counseling.

       RC IV-2   The name and contact information (phone number, web site, etc.) of a translation service for families whose home language is other than English as well as a service that provides American Sign Language translation.

       RC IV-3   The name, contact information and brief descriptions of at least two agencies in the community that provide resources and services for children with disabilities (in most communities, the local school district provides these services).

       RC IV-4   A list of three or more websites, and brief descriptions of each, that provide current information to help families understand how young children develop and learn. Include one current article for each website. Web sites must contain articles that help families understand the development and learning of infants and toddlers. At least one article must relate to child guidance.

RC V   Three samples of **record keeping forms** you use/have used. Include an accident report form, an emergency form and a completed tool/form that you have used to observe for and document a child's developmental/learning progress *(Do not include the child's name).*

RC VI-1 The name and contact information of your state's agency that is responsible for **the regulation of child care centers and family child care homes**. (Note: These regulations are available at the website of the National Resource Center for Health and Safety in Child Care: *http://nrckids.org/STATES/states.htm*). Make a copy of the sections that describe the qualification requirements for personnel (teachers, directors and assistants) and group size, adult-child ratio requirements.

RC VI-2 A list of two or three **early childhood associations** (national, regional, state or local), including website addresses, describing the professional resources and membership opportunities they each offer.

RC VI-3 Summaries of the **legal requirements** in your state regarding child abuse and neglect (including contact information for the appropriate agency in your state) and Mandatory Reporting Guidelines.

The Reflective Statements of Competence

Prepare six written reflections on your own teaching practices. You must write one Reflective Statement for each of the six CDA Competency Standards (see below for specific requirements). Many of the Statements require the use of specific Resources from your *Resource Collection*, above, as the focus of that written reflection. Each Statement should be no more than 500 words in length.

CSI   **Competency Statement I** *(To establish and maintain a safe, healthy learning environment)*:

Begin your Reflective Statement about this Competency Standard with a paragraph describing how your teaching practices meet this Standard (Note: alternatively, you may also choose to write one paragraph for each Functional Area, if this makes it easier to express your thoughts more clearly).

Then write at least one paragraph on each of the following:

CS I a   Reflect on the sample menu in the *Resource Collection* (RC I-2): If you designed the menu, how does it reflect your commitment to children's nutritional needs? If you did not design it, what are its strengths and/or what would you change?

CS I b   Reflect on the room environment in which your CDA Verification Visit™ Observation will occur: How does the room design reflect the way you believe young children learn best? If the room was not designed by you, what do you see as its strengths and/or what would you change?

Additionally, reflect on and describe the similarities and differences between room environments designed for infants as compared to toddlers.

CS I c   Reflect on the weekly plan you included in your *Resource Collection* (RC I-3). How does this plan reflect your philosophy of what young children need on a weekly basis? If the plan was not designed by you, what do you see as its strengths and/or what would you change?

Additionally, describe how you would adapt this weekly plan for use with each of the three age groups (young infants, mobile infants and toddlers).

CSII   **Competency Statement II** *(To advance physical and intellectual competence):*

Begin your Reflective Statement about this Competency Standard with a paragraph describing how your teaching practices meet this Standard (Note: alternatively, you may also choose to write one paragraph for each Functional Area, if this makes it easier to express your thoughts more clearly). Then prepare at least one paragraph on each of the following:

Then prepare at least one paragraph on each of the following:

CS II a   Pick one of the nine learning experiences you chose for your *Resource Collection* (RC II). How does this experience reflect your philosophy of how to support young children's *physical* development?

CS II b   Pick another of the nine learning experiences you chose for your *Resource Collection* (RC II). How does this experience reflect your philosophy of how to support young children's *cognitive* development?

CS II c   Pick a third learning experience you chose for your *Resource Collection* (RC II). How does this experience reflect your philosophy of how to support young children's *creative* development?

CS II d   In an additional paragraph, describe ways to promote the communication/ language development among all children, including dual language learners.

CSIII   **Competency Statement III** *(To support social and emotional development and to provide positive guidance):*

Begin your Reflective Statement about this Competency Standard with a paragraph describing how your teaching practices meet this Standard (Note: alternatively, you may also choose to write one paragraph for each Functional Area, if this makes it easier to express your thoughts more clearly).

Then prepare at least one paragraph on each of the following:

CS III a   Describe some of the ways you support the development of children's positive self-concepts and growing social/emotional skills.

CS III b   Reflect on your philosophy of guiding young children's *positive* behaviors. How is your professional philosophy similar or different from how you were guided as a child? How do you constructively deal with young children's *challenging* behaviors?

CSIV   **Competency Statement IV** *(To establish positive and productive relationships with families)*:

Begin your Reflective Statement about this Competency Standard with a paragraph describing how your teaching practices meet this Standard.

Then prepare at least one paragraph on each of the following:

CS IV a   How do you ensure that families are kept aware of what's happening in their child's daily/weekly life in your program?

CS IV b   How do you ensure that you are aware of what's happening in each child's home life? How does that awareness direct your teaching practices?

CS IV c   Reflect on the feedback you received in the *Family Questionnaires* you collected (please see pp. 12-13). Explain how the responses surprised you, confirmed your own reflections about yourself and/or gave you a new goal for professional growth.

CSV   **Competency Statement V** *(To ensure a well-run, purposeful program that is responsive to participant needs)*:

Begin your Reflective Statement about this Competency Standard with a paragraph describing how your teaching practices meet this Standard.

CS V a   Then write at least one paragraph that describes how you used the observation tool/form you included in the *Resource Collection* (RC V). Why are observation and documentation important parts of program management? How do you ensure that you are accurately/objectively observing and tracking each child's developmental and learning progress?

CSVI   **Competency Statement VI** *(To maintain a commitment to professionalism)*:

Begin your Reflective Statement about this Competency Standard with a paragraph describing how your professional practices meet this Standard. Then:

CS VI a   Reflect on why you chose to become an early childhood professional.

CS VI b   Reflect on what you believe are the most important indicators of professionalism that you possess.

The Professional Philosophy Statement

The *Professional Philosophy Statement* is the final reflective task in the creation of your *Professional Portfolio*. Here you will summarize your professional beliefs and values about early childhood education after you have completed the professional development experience of designing your Portfolio by collecting resources and writing all six *Reflective Statements of Competence*. The *Professional Philosophy Statement* should be no more than two pages in length.

Identify your personal values and beliefs around teaching and learning: How do you believe young children learn? Based on this, what do you believe your role is? Beyond teaching and learning, reflect and write about what you believe are the other important aspects of your role in the lives of children and families.

Bring Your Professional Portfolio to your CDA Verification Visit™!

Once you have completed the preparation of your *Professional Portfolio*, please hold on to it until your CDA Verification Visit™, at which time your PD Specialist will review it.

Note: You are required to present your Portfolio to your PD Specialist at the time of your CDA Verification Visit™. Please do not send your Professional Portfolio to the Council at any time. The Council will not return any portfolios.

Apply for the CDA Credentialing Process

Identify a CDA Professional Development Specialist and obtain her or his identification number.

The application requires you to identify a CDA Professional Development (PD) Specialist who will agree to conduct your CDA Verification Visit™. Once the PD Specialist agrees, she/he will provide you with her/his Identification Number. You will need to include this number in your application.

- Identify a CDA Professional Development Specialist and obtain her or his Identification Number

- Secure your director's permission for your CDA Verification Visit™

- Submit the CDA application to the Council and pay the assessment fee

The Council uses the PD Specialist Identification Number to ensure that you have chosen a PD Specialist who has been trained by the Council and is currently available to conduct CDA Verification Visits™ in your area. The Council will process your application only after confirming that you have identified an appropriate PD Specialist to conduct your CDA Verification Visit™.

Finding a Professional Development Specialist

There are four ways to find a Professional Development Specialist:

- Ask someone you know who already is a PD Specialist

- Ask an early childhood professional in your community to become a PD Specialist, directing them to *www.cdacouncil.org/pds* to apply for and take an online training to serve in the role

Note: If you choose options 1 or 2, please give careful, ethical consideration to the Council's Conflicts of Interest policy on the next page.

- Go to *www.cdacouncil.org/findapds* to use the Find-a-PD Specialist online tool, which will send a request on your behalf to a local PD Specialist.

- If none of the above methods work, you may call the Council at 800-424-4310

PD Specialist Eligibility Requirements

A wide range of experienced early childhood professionals may serve as CDA Professional Development Specialists. Please see p. 116 for the complete list of PD Specialist eligibility requirements.

PD Specialist Conflicts of Interest

Although a particular individual may meet all of the general eligibility requirements to become a PD Specialist, you and your prospective PD Specialist must decide, together, if there are any ethical conflicts of interests related to your relationship that may disqualify her/him from serving as your PD Specialist.

No person may serve as your PD Specialist if she/he is:

1. your immediate relative (mother, father, sibling, spouse, son, daughter)
2. your current direct supervisor
3. A co-worker in same group/classroom that you work

If you are in any of these three types of relationships with this person, you may not, under any circumstances, choose this person as your PD Specialist.

However, there are many other types of relationships that will require both you and your prospective PD Specialist to consider carefully. Positions of a prospective PD Specialist that bear ethical consideration by you both are:

- Indirect supervisor
- Trainer, either indirect or direct
- Any person or representative of an organization that has financial/contractual considerations related to you or may benefit in any way from your credentialing outcome
- Your employer
- A co-employee in the same facility, not in the same group/classroom
- A peer/friend
- Any person who may have a personal or professional bias toward or against you or any group of which you are a part
- A licensing agent

The Council will not exclude any person with a relationship that may fall in one or more of the categories in the "ethical considerations" list, above, from applying, but reserves the right to enact further inquiries and end the service of a PD Specialist and/or application of a Candidate at any time should a question of conflict arise. Please note that every PD Specialist and Candidate will both be asked to sign a Statement of Ethics.

Secure your director's permission for your CDA Verification Visit™

The application requires the signature of your center/program director to confirm the following:

- The CDA Verification Visit™ can happen during the center/program's work hours.

- The PD Specialist will be allowed to observe you working with children in your classroom.

- During the CDA Verification Visit™, you can be observed leading children's activities.

- You and your PD Specialist will be provided a quiet space if you are planning to complete the Review and/or Reflect sessions of your CDA Verification Visit™ on the premises of your center/program.

Complete the CDA application

Apply online at *cdacouncil.org/yourcda*. If you do not have online access, you may use the paper application found at the end of this book.

In the online or paper application, you will confirm that you have completed all preparation requirements found on pp. 10-20 of this book. You will also choose the language of your CDA Exam (English or Spanish, regardless of the language you choose for your CDA Verification Visit™). To ensure a speedy and smooth credentialing process, follow the directions closely and do not skip any portion of the application.

Please be sure to carefully complete each section of your application and to sign it at the end. Failure to complete any part of the application will result in delayed processing times as the Council must then return the application to you for correction. The Council cannot guarantee a timely credentialing decision if you do not properly complete your application. If you have missing information in your application, the Council will inform you and

Apply Online!

The *YourCDA®* online application, found at *cdacouncil.org/yourcda* is simple and easy to use. Applying for your credential online will significantly speed up your credentialing process. Using the *YourCDA®* online application you can:

- Save your work and continue later

- Check your status anytime

- Pay the assessment fee electronically

- Communicate quickly with the Council

- Get automatic updates as to where you are in the credentialing process

Look for this icon

 Your CDA®

at cdacouncil.org to learn more

give you 60 days to correct it, after which time you will forfeit your assessment fee and will need to start the credentialing process over, including the payment of a new assessment fee.

Note: If you change your name and/or address any time after you submit your CDA application, please inform the Council as soon as possible so that, if you are awarded the CDA credential, you can be certain that the Council prints your name accordingly.

The current assessment fee can be found on the application and on the Council's website, _cdacouncil.org_.

You must submit the complete assessment fee with your application. You may pay the assessment fee via credit card, check, money order or agency scholarship. If you pay with an agency scholarship, you will need to provide documentation of this scholarship through a payment authorization letter from the agency.

Email Will Speed up Your CDA Credentialing Process!

Don't yet have an email address? Don't spend another day out of the loop! You can get a free email account through many different online providers including gmail.com, yahoo.com and hotmail.com.

If the Council has your correct email address, you will receive:

- The *Ready to Schedule* notice, once your CDA application is reviewed and approved by the Council

- Reminders to schedule your CDA Verification Visit™ and CDA Exam before the six-month deadline

- A renewal reminder before your CDA Credential expires

- Updates about any important changes to the CDA process and Council services

- The CounciLINK monthly e-newsletter, filled with valuable resources and news for the national CDA Community

Demonstrate Your Competence

After the Council has processed your application and payment, you will receive a *Ready to Schedule* notification. This will be sent via email if you provided an email address or by mail if you did not.

Note: If you provided an email address, the email notification will come from the following email address: *cdaready@cdacouncil.org*. Please add this address to your email address book to ensure that your notification is delivered to your Inbox, rather than your Junk Mail/Spam Folder.

③ Demonstrate ➤

Once the Council has approved your application and processed your payment, you must schedule and complete the following:

- Your CDA Verification Visit™
- Your CDA Exam

You may complete your CDA Verification Visit™ and take the CDA Exam as quickly as you would like and in whichever order works best for you. However, **you must complete both within six months** from the date of your *Ready to Schedule* notice. If you do not complete your CDA Exam and CDA Verification Visit™ within six months, you will forfeit your application fee and your Candidate record will be closed. If this happens, you will need to begin the CDA Credentialing process from the beginning and pay a new assessment fee.

The CDA Verification Visit™

Scheduling Your CDA Verification Visit™

When you receive your *Ready to Schedule* notification, your PD Specialist will also receive an email notifying her/him that you are ready to schedule your CDA Verification Visit™. While your PD Specialist will be required to make contact with you within five business days, the Council encourages you to take ownership of your credentialing process by reaching out to her/him first. Together you will then determine the date and time for your CDA Verification Visit™. Please be sure to confirm these arrangements with your Director. Once confirmed, you may find it helpful to write the date and time in the appropriate space on the Candidate Checklist, found on the inside front cover of this book.

You must bring the following items to your CDA Verification Visit™:

- Your original, complete Professional Portfolio, including all of the required contents listed on the *Professional Portfolio* cover sheet (found at the end of this book):
  - Transcripts, certificates, documentation of your professional education
  - *Family Questionnaires*
  - *Resource Collection*
  - *Six Reflective Statements of Competence*
  - *Professional Philosophy Statement*
- This *Competency Standards* book, including:
  - The blank *Comprehensive Scoring Instrument* your PD Specialist will use (found at the end of this book)
  - The *Reflective Dialogue* worksheet (also found at the end of this book), with the "Areas of Strength" and "Areas for Professional Growth" boxes from the *Family Questionnaires* completed

Rescheduling Your CDA Verification Visit™

Any time prior to the CDA Verification Visit™, you and/or your PD Specialist may reschedule the CDA Verification Visit™. If you cannot agree on a new date and time for the CDA Verification Visit™, you may find a different PD Specialist without penalty. You must contact the Council and give the Council the ID number of the new PD Specialist prior to the rescheduled CDA Verification Visit™.

If your PD Specialist arrives for your CDA Verification Visit™ and you are not there within 15 minutes of the scheduled time, she/he will record your CDA Verification Visit™ as a "no-show". If this happens, you cannot earn a CDA Credential until you reschedule your Visit with that PD Specialist or find another PD Specialist to complete your CDA Verification Visit™ within your initial six-month window. In order to do this you must first contact the Council at 800-424-4310 for authorization. At that time, you will be required to pay an additional $125 fee (which covers the PD Specialist honorarium from the first Visit as well as Council processing costs).

Meeting All Requirements

If your PD Specialist determines that you did not meet either of the requirements of a) your professional education documentation or b) your First Aid/Pediatric CPR, she/he will inform you at the completion of your CDA Verification Visit™. Shortly thereafter, you will receive a postcard from the Council notifying you of the required procedures for correcting these errors within six months of your Ready to Schedule notice. If you do not correct these requirements within this time frame, you will forfeit your assessment fee and will need to start the credentialing process over, including the payment of a new assessment fee.

Your CDA Verification Visit™

At your CDA Verification Visit™, your PD Specialist will utilize the R.O.R Model™ to verify key aspects of your professional competency. "R.O.R." stands for Review-Observe-Reflect™. During the CDA Verification Visit™, the Specialist will:

Review *the contents of your Professional Portfolio.* You will need to ensure that your PD Specialist has a quiet space, with a tabletop surface, where she/he can review your materials for sixty minutes.

Observe *you working with children.* The PD Specialist will sit silently observing you leading program activities with children for two hours. You must work with your PD Specialist in advance to ensure that you schedule the observation for a two-hour window in which the children will be awake and that you will be working with them the entire time.

Reflect *with you.* After the Review and Observe sessions, you will meet with your PD Specialist for a reflective dialogue in which you will discuss your areas of strength or growth, for the purpose of setting professional goals. This reflective dialogue, though required, has no influence on whether or not you earn the CDA Credential. It is provided to support your professional growth and will follow a specific, set agenda (please see pp. 118-120). Any goals you may set will be yours, privately, and will not be sent to the Council. However, the Council encourages you to share your goals with a trusted peer, mentor or even your supervisor. Research shows that professionals are more likely to meet the goals they have set for themselves when they have another person to offer support and hold them accountable.

During the Visit, the Specialist will use the Comprehensive Scoring Instrument at the back of this book to determine Recommended Scores for

> In coordination with your PD Specialist, you have the flexibility to schedule the one hour **Review** of materials any time before or after the two hour **Observation**.
>
> The **Reflect** session must occur last – either immediately following the Observation or Review Sessions, later in the day (for example, during Nap Time) or on another day that week (for example, on Saturday).
>
> However, all three Sessions must be completed *within 7 consecutive days*.

each of the 51 Items in each of the thirteen Functional Areas found on pp. 39-106 in this book, using a combination of evidence found in your Professional Portfolio and through her/his observation of you working with children.

The PD Specialist will then submit Recommended Scores to the Council online within 48 hours of your CDA Verification Visit™. These scores, along with the CDA Exam score, will be combined by the Council into a final Cumulative Score which will determine your credentialing decision.

The CDA Exam

After you receive your *Ready to Schedule* notice (which will include your Candidate ID number), you may proceed to schedule your CDA Exam. You will take the computer-based exam at a local Pearson Vue testing center. Note: There is no additional fee to take your CDA Exam.

Scheduling Your CDA Exam

Scheduling your exam is very simple. You must contact Pearson Vue directly, via website or phone. Note: the Council is not able to schedule the CDA Exam for you.

Scheduling with Pearson Vue Online:

1. Go to *www.pearsonvue.com/cdaexam*

2. Click on the *Schedule an Exam* button on the right side of your screen

3. Click on the *Create a Web Account* link

4. Enter the Candidate ID number which you received with your *Ready to Schedule* notice from the Council (Note: You will not able to proceed without providing this number therefore you cannot schedule your CDA Exam until you have received your *Ready to Schedule* notice)

5. Verify that all of your personal information is correct (Note: if any of your information is incorrect, please contact the Council immediately at 800-424-4310)

6. Set up your username and password, writing them down on your Candidate Checklist, found on the inside front cover of this book

7. Once you have created your Pearson Vue Web Account, you may return to *www.pearsonvue.com/cdaexam* at any time to find a testing center nearest to you based on your zip code, schedule, cancel or reschedule your CDA Exam.

If you create your Pearson Vue account online...

...you will be able to find the test center closest to you, look at its calendar and choose a convenient day and time for your exam. You will be able to access your account any time to get directions to the test center and to cancel or reschedule your exam.

Scheduling with Pearson Vue over the Phone:

1. Call 866-507-5627 (8:00 a.m. to 8:00 p.m. EST M-F)

2. Tell the operator your Candidate ID number or your name and that you wish to schedule the CDA Exam.

3. Verify that all of your personal information is correct (Note: if any of your information is incorrect, please contact the Council immediately at 800-424-4310)

4. Tell the operator where and when you wish to take the CDA Exam. The operator will assist you in finding the closest exam location.

Note: Military Candidates who wish to schedule their exam at their base should do so at *www.pearsonvue.com/military*.

After you schedule your CDA Exam, you will receive a *Confirmation Note* from Pearson Vue with the location and date you chose for your CDA Exam. The confirmation will also include the address, phone number and directions to the test center you chose. Write down the address and phone number on your Candidate Checklist, found on the inside front cover of this book.

> ### Set Yourself Up for Success!
>
> Choose an exam location and date that are most convenient for you. Before you choose the test center, make sure to investigate its location, accessibility and availability of parking (review the information presented on the website or ask Pearson Vue when calling). Calculate the amount of time you will need to get to the center and choose your appointment time accordingly.
>
> You must arrive at the test center at least 15 minutes before your appointment time. Estimate how much time it will take you to get to the center. If you arrive late, you may not be able to take the exam.

Rescheduling Your CDA Exam

If you need to reschedule the CDA Exam, you must first cancel your current appointment before you can schedule another appointment. Pearson Vue will charge you a $15 cancellation fee each time you cancel the scheduled CDA exam. You may only use a credit card or debit card to pay the cancellation fee. You may cancel and reschedule your exam appointment via your Pearson Vue online account or you may call Pearson Vue at 866-507-5627 (8:00 a.m. to 8:00 p.m. EST M-F).

You will not be allowed to cancel within 24 hours of your scheduled exam. If you miss your scheduled exam, Pearson Vue will require an additional $65 for a second exam. The Candiate can pay the $65 with credit/debt card only. No checks will be accepted. In order to do this you must first contact the Council at 800-424-4310 for authorization.

If severe weather or a natural disaster makes the test center inaccessible or unsafe, the examination will be delayed or canceled without penalty to you. Call Pearson Vue at 866-507-5627 or call the test center directly for details on delays and cancellations during severe weather.

Preparing for Your CDA Exam

The CDA Exam covers practical examples of early childhood best practices; the material found in the CDA Competency Standards and Functional Areas. Your 120 hours of professional education and 480 hours working with young children should prepare you for the Exam. For a refresher, you might review the Competency Standards section of this book and "CDA Exam Questions" on pp. 121-122.

Taking Your CDA Exam

You will be able to take the CDA Exam only one time during your credentialing process.

Before the Exam Begins

The Exam will be presented to you in English or Spanish, depending on the choice you indicated on your CDA application. Before the exam begins, the computer program will give you 15 minutes to review instructions, to agree to the required Nondisclosure Agreement, and to practice clicking with your mouse by answering three practice questions.

You will then have one hour and 45 minutes to complete the exam, however most Candidates find that they are able to complete the Exam in an hour or less. Note: the computer program will remind you when you have 30 minutes and 10 minutes left.

The CDA Exam has 65 multiple choice questions including five that

Rules and Procedures at Pearson Vue Testing Centers

• A valid photo ID will be required to take your Exam. The photo ID must include your signature. The photo ID you present at the test center must match the name you included on your CDA application. If, for example, you got married or divorced since the time you completed your application to the Council, you must bring a marriage certificate or divorce decree with you to the test center.

• You will be asked to sign a required agreement to follow Pearson Vue's test-taking rules.

• Before entering the testing room, the Pearson Vue proctor will ask you to leave all of your personal belongings outside the testing room, in a locker or your car.

• Your friends or relatives will not be able to wait for you in the waiting area.

• You may get up to use the bathroom during the exam, but your timer will continue to run.

• Always raise your hand if you need assistance of any kind. Do not hesitate to ask for help if you are experiencing technical problems.

• There will be other test takers in the room with you. Always be respectful and try not to disrupt others.

have a photo and a brief classroom scenario. The questions will be presented to you one at a time. You may freely move between questions, choosing and changing your answers, as long as time permits.

The CDA Exam has been designed to be easy-to-take for those new to computers. You will only need to know how to point and single click a mouse in order to complete the Exam.

Try to answer all the questions, even if you have to guess. Questions that are left unanswered will be marked as wrong. If you are not sure of the best answer, you may "flag" the question to come back to later. After you have viewed all of the 65 questions, you will be shown a "Review" screen. The Review screen is a summary of all of your answers including the questions you did not answer (incomplete) and which questions you flagged to come back to later. If time permits, you may go back and answer the questions you flagged or did not answer. When you are ready, click "End the Review". Once you do this, you will no longer be able to go back to review or change your answers.

> ## Exam Tutorial
>
> The Council has created a tutorial to help you learn how to use the various functions of the CDA Exam screens.
>
> You will find the tutorial by visiting *cdacouncil.org/CDAexam/tutorial*.

When you are done, you must click the "End Exam" button before leaving the testing room. Your exam answers will then be immediately transmitted to the Council for Professional Recognition.

Your CDA Exam scores, along with your CDA Verification Visit™ Recommended Scores, submitted by your Professional Development Specialist, will be combined by the Council into a final Cumulative Score which will determine your credentialing decision.

Earn Your CDA Credential

After the Council receives the scores for both your CDA Verification Visit™ and your CDA Exam, the Council creates a Cumulative Score in order to determine your final credentialing decision.

The Cumulative Score takes into account your understanding of the six CDA Competency Standards and 13 Functional Areas (Part 2 of this book) and your ability to put them into practice. There is not a passing or failing score on either the

- **Earn your CDA Credential**
- **Renew your CDA Credential**
- **Earn a second CDA Credential**

CDA Exam or the CDA Verification Visit™. Rather, the Council comprehensively evaluates how you score in each of the Functional Areas during the CDA Verification Visit™ and on the CDA Exam to arrive at its decision. As a result, you will not receive a score after you have taken your CDA Exam or after the CDA Verification Visit™.

If the Council determines that your Cumulative Score meets the credentialing requirement, you will be awarded the Child Development Associate® (CDA) Credential™. If the Council determines that your Cumulative Score does not meet the credentialing requirement, the Council will notify you and inform you of appeal procedures and other subsequent options.

If you earn your CDA, the Council will mail your credential to the address listed on your application.

Renew Your Credential

A CDA Credential is valid for three years from the date of award. You may apply to renew your CDA credential six months before it expires. In order to renew your CDA Credential you will need to provide:

- Proof of your valid and current certificates of completion or cards from a) any Face-to-Face first aid course and b) an infant/child (pediatric) CPR course offered by a nationally-recognized training organization (such as American Red Cross or the American Heart Association). *Online training is not accepted.*

- Proof of professional education training specific to **original** credential setting: at least 4.5 Continuing Education Units (CEUs) or a three-credit-hour course in early childhood education/child development (these hours must be completed after original 120 clock hours you obtained in order to earn your initial CDA Credential. You have already earned your initial CDA, as you prepare for CDA renewal your professional development and training courses must enhance your basic knowledge and skills. **You should not re-take**

the exact same courses you studied when applying for your original credential.

- Proof of a minimum of 80 hours of recent work experience with young children specific to the original credential setting (within the current year).

- A completed Letter of Recommendation form from an early childhood professional regarding your current skills in working with young children specific to the original credential setting (this form can be found in the CDA Renewal Procedures Guide, which is available for download from our website.)

- Proof of current membership in a national or local early childhood professional organization

To learn more about CDA Renewal, please visit cdacouncil.org/renewal or view the CDA Renewal Procedures *www.cdacouncil.org/renew*.

Earn a Second Credential

Candidates wishing to earn a CDA credential of another type (Infant/Toddler, Preschool, Family Child Care or Home Visitor) must complete the CDA credentialing process again. All steps must be completed and you must submit a new assessment fee. However, to meet the requirement of 120 hours of professional education, you may re-use the portions of your professional education that relate to the second credential type (for example, a class titled "Working with Families" could be re-used for any credential type whereas a class titled "Infant Emotional Development" could not be re-used for the Preschool CDA Credential).

Language Specializations

Bilingual Language Specialization (English and a Second Language)

A bilingual program is a child development program that has specific goals for promoting bilingual development in children, in which two languages are consistently used in daily activities and in which families are helped to understand the goals and support children's bilingual development.

A bilingual Candidate is a Candidate who works in this type of program and is required to use both languages daily and consistently with children and their families and who is able to speak, read and write both languages well enough to understand and be understood by others in both English and the second language.

In addition to all of the competencies being assessed in the standard credentialing process, Candidates seeking Bilingual Specialization are also assessed in their ability to promote and facilitate children's bilingual development through consistent use of both languages in daily activities, as required by her/his job in a bilingual program.

Although there is no specific model of bilingual education that this Candidate should follow, a competent Candidate is knowledgeable about the development of language, bilingual communication, and the integration of culture and language. The Candidate should have specific strategies for achieving bilingual development and be able to implement them through consistent daily opportunities where children build on their first language and culture, while learning the second language. This may include programs where children who speak English are learning a second language.

① Prepare

Since being added to the CDA credentialing process in 1979, the CDA Bilingual assessment requirements have been developed so that Candidates working in bilingual programs could demonstrate their special competencies in order to earn a CDA Credential with a Bilingual Specialization. Special, required bilingual examples of competence are now woven into 11 of the 13 Functional Areas, with the exception of "Healthy" and "Physical". The examples are not inclusive - Candidates may think of many additional examples of competent behavior for bilingual early care and learning professionals.

Education Requirements

Candidates applying for Bilingual Specialization are required to study Principles of Dual Language Learning (pp. 109-115) as part of their hours of study under Subject Area #2:"Advancing children's physical and intellectual development". Therefore, in addition to providing verification of completion of 120 clock hours of education in the form of a transcript, certificate or letter, these Candidates must include a course description or syllabus specific and pertinent to a Principles of Dual Language Learning course of study.

The Professional Portfolio

In addition to meeting all of the standard requirements for Professional Portfolios, Bilingual Specialization requires:

Family Questionnaires

When inviting families to complete the Family Questionnaires, families should be asked to complete all questions, paying particular attention to Question #14, which is specific to bilingual programs.

The Resource Collection

The resources used directly with children and families must be presented in both languages (RC I-3, RC II, RC III, RC IV)

Reflective Statements of Competence

Three statements must be written in English and three in the other language (the Candidate may select which ones). All six Statements of Competence must include information in regards to how Candidate applies principles of Dual Language Learning to her bilingual daily practice with children.

Professional Philosophy Statement

The Candidate may write the Professional Philosophy Statement in either language.

 Apply

Candidates who wish to apply for a Bilingual Specialization may do so using a combination of English and any other language. Note: If you are interested in applying for a Bilingual Specialization in any language other than Spanish, please call the Council at 800-424-4310 to discuss special arrangements.

This *Competency Standards* book is also available in Spanish, including the application, the Comprehensive Scoring Instrument and all resources. At this time, the Council does not offer these materials in other languages.

Demonstrate

The CDA Verification Visit™

The Candidate must utilize a Professional Development (PD) Specialist who is proficient in both languages (able to speak, read and write English and the other language) and can understand and be understood by both children and adults. The PD Specialist must have direct experience with Bilingual Early Childhood programs and with non-English speaking populations. The PD Specialist will conduct the reflective dialogue with the Candidate in both languages.

The Observation held during the CDA Verification Visit™ must take place in an eligible bilingual program and must reflect the Candidate's work using both languages daily and consistently.

 Candidates seeking Bilingual Specialization must also display competence in additional required examples found throughout the *Competency Standards* as denoted by the special icon on the left.

The CDA Exam

The CDA Exam may be taken by all Candidates in either English or Spanish. Candidates applying for a Bilingual Specialization of English and a language other than Spanish will take the Exam in English.

Monolingual Language Specialization

In addition to meeting all of the standard requirements for earning the CDA Credential, Candidates applying for a Monolingual Specialization must meet the following requirements. Note: If the language of the Specialization is other than Spanish, the Candidate must contact the Council before applying in order to discuss special arrangements.

Prepare

The Professional Portfolio

In addition to meeting all of the standard requirements for Professional Portfolios, Monolingual Specialization requires:

Family Questionnaires

Family Questionnaires may be completed in either language by families.

The Resource Collection

The resources used directly with children and families must be presented in Spanish (RC I-3, RC II, RC III, RC IV)

Reflective Statements of Competence

All statements must be written in Spanish.

Professional Philosophy Statement

The Candidate must write the Professional Philosophy Statement in Spanish.

3 Demonstrate

The CDA Verification Visit™

The Candidate must select a Professional Development (PD) Specialist who is proficient in Spanish.

The Observation must take place in an eligible monolingual setting and must reflect the Candidate's work using Spanish language daily and consistently

The PD Specialist will conduct the reflective dialogue with the Candidate in Spanish.

The CDA Exam

The CDA Exam may be taken by all Candidates, including Monolingual Candidates, in either English or Spanish. Candidates applying for a Monolingual Specialization in a language other than Spanish must contact the Council for special arrangements.

Part 2

The Child Development Associate® Competency Standards

I. To establish and maintain a safe, healthy learning environment

II. To advance physical and intellectual competence

III. To support social and emotional development and provide positive guidance

IV. To establish positive and productive relationships with families

V. To ensure a well-run, purposeful program that is responsive to participant needs

VI. To maintain a commitment to professionalism

The Child Development Associate® Competency Standards

Candidates seeking to earn the CDA Credential are assessed based upon the CDA Competency Standards. These national standards are the criteria used to evaluate an early care and learning professional's performance with children, families, colleagues and their community.

There are six *Competency Standards* - statements that set the standard of competency for professional behavior. The first four Standards relate directly to the experiences of young children and are therefore presented within a *Developmental Context*. Each Developmental Context presents a brief overview of relevant child development principles related to the Functional Areas within that Standard.

The six Standards are then defined in more detail in 13 *Functional Areas*, which describe the major tasks or functions that an early care and learning professional must complete in order to meet each Competency Standard. Each Functional Area includes *Items* that further define it as well as *Indicators* that further delineate each Item. Additionally, most Items have a list of optional *Examples* to further illustrate key professional practices. The Examples are not intended to be all-inclusive as individual teaching styles, cultural norms and program needs vary. It is likely that Candidates, CDA Professional Development Specialists and other readers may think of many more examples, in addition to the ones listed.

Examples have also been provided for certain Items that are unique to Bilingual Specialization. Please refer to "Principles for Dual Language Learners" (pp. 107-113) for additional principles that provide guidance for working with preschool children whose primary (home) language is not English. A description of the developmental components of dual language acquisition emphasizes the importance of competent practices that support constructive dual language development of preschool children. Multiple examples of competent practice are presented.

Competent early care and learning professionals integrate their work and constantly adapt their skills, always thinking of the development of the whole child. In all Functional Areas, it is important for these professionals to individualize their work with each child while meeting the needs of the group. Additionally, professionals must display cultural competence, supporting children and families of varied cultural groups as well as meeting the unique needs of children with special needs. Competent professionals must also demonstrate personal qualities, such as flexibility and a positive style of communicating with young children and working with families.

Navigating the CDA Competency Standards

Universal Standards

The Standards, Functional Areas, Items and Indicators are universal (i.e, they apply to Infant/ Toddler, Preschool and Family Child Care settings). However, the Examples are based on children's developmental levels and may vary by Credential type (in other words, some of the Infant/toddler examples found in this book may be different than the preschool examples found in the *Preschool Competency Standards* book).

Hierarchy of the Standards

Key to the Hierarchy of the CDA Competency Standards:

Competency Standard

Functional Area

Item / Item / Item

a) Indicator

• Example

Organization of Items

For ease-of use by the CDA Professional Development Specialist, the Items on the following pages have been color-coded to match the way they will be reviewed and observed using the Comprehensive Scoring Instrument at the back of this book:

Settings & Activities

Actions & Interactions

Review

Bilingual Specialization

 Indicates a required example for Candidates seeking Bilingual Specialization

Infant/Toddler Competency Standards At-A-Glance

Competency Standard	Functional Area	Definitions
I. To establish and maintain a safe, healthy learning environment	1. Safe	Candidate provides a safe environment to prevent and reduce injuries.
	2. Healthy	Candidate promotes good health and nutrition and provides an environment that contributes to the prevention of illness.
	3. Learning Environment	Candidate uses space, relationships, materials, and routines as resources for constructing an interesting, secure and enjoyable environment that encourages and fosters trust, play, exploration, interaction and learning.
II. To advance physical and intellectual competence	4. Physical	Candidate uses a variety of developmentally appropriate equipment, learning experiences and teaching strategies to promote the physical development (fine motor and gross motor) of all children.
	5. Cognitive	Candidate provides activities and opportunities that encourage curiosity, exploration and problem-solving appropriate to the developmental levels of each child.
	6. Communication	Candidate actively communicates with children and provides opportunities and support for children to understand, acquire and to use verbal and nonverbal means of communicating thoughts and feelings.
	7. Creative	Candidate provides opportunities that encourage children to play with sound, rhythm, language, materials, space and ideas in individual ways and to express their creative abilities.
III. To support social and emotional development and to provide positive guidance	8. Self	Candidate develops a warm, positive, supportive and responsive relationship with each child and helps each child learn about and take pride in his or her individual and cultural identities.
	9. Social	Candidate helps each child feel accepted in the group, helps children learn to communicate and get along with others and encourages feelings of empathy and mutual respect among children and adults.
	10. Guidance	Candidate provides a supportive environment and uses effective strategies to help all children learn and practice appropriate and acceptable behaviors as individuals and as a group, and effectively provides support for children with persistent challenging behaviors.
IV. To establish positive and productive relationships with families	11. Families	Candidate establishes a positive, responsive, cooperative relationship with each child's family, engages in two-way communication with families, encourages their involvement in the program and supports the child's relationship with her/his family.
V. To ensure a well-run, purposeful program that is responsive to participant needs	12. Program Management	Candidate is a manager who uses all available resources to ensure an effective program operation. Candidate is a competent organizer, record keeper, communicator and cooperative co-worker.
VI. To maintain a commitment to professionalism	13. Professionalism	Candidate makes decisions based on knowledge of research-based early childhood practices, promotes high-quality in child care services and takes advantage of opportunities to improve knowledge and competence, both for personal and professional growth and for the benefit of children and families.

Competency Standard I:

To establish and maintain a safe, healthy learning environment

Developmental Contexts

Safe:

Young and mobile infants *(birth–17 months)* need affectionate and competent physical care geared to their individual needs and rhythms. Adults can help infants regulate their eating, sleeping and other activities gradually, while continuing to balance the infant's and the group's needs.

Toddlers *(18–36 months)* imitate and learn from the activities of those around them. Good health habits can be established through modeling and encouraging handwashing, nutritious eating, etc. Toddlers are increasingly curious about their world. They stretch boundaries and test everything in their surroundings. Adults must be attentive to their activities and ensure their safety while giving them simple explanations for safety precautions.

Healthy:

Young and mobile infants *(birth–17 months)* need affectionate and competent physical care geared to their individual needs and rhythms. Adults individualize infants' eating, sleeping and other daily routines, while continuing to balance the infant's and the group's needs.

Toddlers *(18–36 months)* imitate and learn from those around them. Good health habits can be established through modeling and encouraging handwashing, nutritious eating, etc.

Learning Environment:

Young infants *(birth–8 months)* are learning from their immediate surroundings and daily experiences with a few important people. The sense of well-being and emotional security conveyed by a loving and skilled caregiver creates a readiness for other experiences. Before infants can creep and crawl, adults should provide a variety of sensory experiences and encourage movement and playfulness.

Mobile infants *(9–17 months)* are active, independent and curious. They are increasingly persistent and purposeful in doing things. They need many opportunities to practice new skills and explore the environment within safe boundaries. Adults can share children's delight in themselves, their skills and discoveries and gradually add variety to the learning environment that will continue to foster relationships and exploration.

Toddlers *(18–36 months)* are developing new language skills, physical control and awareness of themselves and others each day. They enjoy participating in planned and group activities, but they are not yet ready to sit still or work in a group for a very long time. Adults can support their learning in all areas by maintaining an environment that is dependable but flexible enough to provide opportunities for them to extend their skills, understanding and judgment in individualized ways.

Functional Area 1: Safe

Candidate provides a safe environment to prevent and reduce injuries.

Item 1.1 Environments are safe for all children and adults.

Indicator:

a) **Materials, equipment and environments are safe**

Examples

- Indoor and outdoor play areas are in good repair, free of debris, structural hazards, splinters, unguarded space heaters, tools, etc.

- Dangerous substances are not in children's reach (such as anything labeled "keep out of reach of children," medicine, cleaning products, matches, chipping paint, toxic plants, small objects that could be swallowed, balloons and plastic bags)

- Indoor and outdoor playground equipment is cushioned with pads or other materials thick enough to prevent injuries

- Toys and equipment are unbreakable, too large to swallow and meet current safety standards

- Safety equipment (such as fire extinguishers and smoke detectors) is in place and operable

- All children's materials are non-toxic, non-flammable and/or water-based

- Furnishings are appropriate for children's development and size

- Outlets are covered with safety caps or other safety devices

- Cords on electronics and window coverings are out of children's reach

- Heating or a/c units are secured and/or inaccessible to children

- Walls and furniture do not have sharp edges

- Rugs and all carpeting lie flat, have non-skid backing or are secured to the floor where necessary

- Exits are properly marked and unobstructed

- Cribs are free of large/heavy blankets, pillows or bumper pads that could restrict a child's breathing

- Side rails on cribs are locked in the "up" position when children are napping

- Crib slats are secure and in good repair

1.2 Well-planned and well-organized emergency procedures and supplies are evident.

a) Procedures for fires and other emergencies are posted

Examples

- A list of current phone numbers for contacting parents and emergency services (poison control, fire stations, police, ambulance/medical help) is accessible

- Posted emergency instructions use diagrams, pictures and words to effectively convey procedures to children, families and staff

- A written evacuation plan is posted

b) First-aid supplies and medicines are stored appropriately and accessible to adults only

Examples

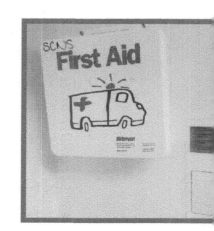

- A first aid kit is evident in the classroom

- A portable first aid kit is available to be taken to the playground and on neighborhood walks, field trips

- Unique first aid equipment and medicines are available for authorized children (such as an EpiPen for children with asthma)

- Medicines are labeled and stored as indicated, out-of-reach of children

1.3 Candidate ensures children's safety at all times.

a) Ensures that children are attended by authorized adults at all times

Examples

- Does not leave children alone with an unauthorized adult

- Knows basic first aid and CPR procedures appropriate for young children (for example, how to handle choking or treating cuts)

- Releases each child only to authorized individuals

b) Teaches children appropriate safety practices

Examples

- Teaches toddlers how to safely use equipment (climbing structures, ride on toys, etc.)

- Regularly practices effective procedures for fires and other emergencies, including safety procedures for children with special needs

- Uses appropriate language to help toddlers understand what behaviors are safe and what might cause harm to themselves, others or the materials

 Candidates seeking Bilingual Specialization must also show evidence of the following:

- Explains and practices safety procedures (for example, fire drills) using the language best understood by the children

c) Provides attentive supervision at all times

Examples

- Supervises all children's activities indoors and outdoors

- Takes safety precautions in a reassuring manner without making children fearful

- Handles emergencies in a reassuring manner without making children fearful

- Uses safe auto and bus travel procedures, including appropriate use of car seats and/or safety belts

- Stays physically close to infants and toddlers

- Maintains physical contact with infants on changing table or when bathing (even if they are strapped in)

- Stores diapering supplies in immediate access to changing table

- Holds toddlers' hands when near dangerous areas (for example, streets, deep water, curbs or steps)

- Secures children in strollers/buggies for walks

- Uses "safe spots" or "safe zones" to keep young infants safe from mobile children

- Places young infants on their backs to sleep to prevent Sudden Infant Death Syndrome (SIDS)

- Knows mobile infants' and toddlers' individual tendencies to bite, climb, escape, etc. Watches or stays close to these children to anticipate and respond quickly

d) Makes sure foods that are known choking hazards are not served

Example

- Small foods that may cause choking (such as hot dog or other cut-up meat pieces, grapes, popcorn, nuts, marshmallows, gummi candies, hard candies, seeds, cherries, etc.) are not served

Functional Area 2: Healthy

Candidate promotes good health and nutrition and provides an environment that contributes to the prevention of illness.

Item 2.1 Children's settings promote good health.

Indicator:

a) Materials, equipment and environments are clean and promote good health

Examples

- Play areas and materials are clean

- Covered, plastic-lined containers are available for used tissues, diapers or other biohazards

b) Disinfecting and sanitizing solutions are present and stored appropriately

Examples

- Chemical air fresheners and scented products are not used

- Bleach/water solution is used to disinfect and sanitize surfaces and materials

- Cleaning supplies are stored in dated, labeled containers, out of children's reach and separated from foods and medicines

c) Relevant health information from families of children are maintained and posted

Examples

- Children's current food allergies are posted (when applicable)

- Current emergency telephone numbers for each child's parent(s), nearest relative and medical providers are easily accessible

- Health records, medication and first aid administration procedures/forms are available

2.2 Candidate implements appropriate hygiene practices to minimize the spread of infectious diseases.

a) Cleans/sanitizes materials and equipment

Examples

- Wipes down all surfaces used by children (tables, furniture, countertops, etc.)

- Sweeps/mops floors
- Follows procedures for cleaning, sanitizing and disinfecting toys and materials
- Removes "mouthed" objects from the play area
- Cleans and sanitizes, at least daily, all toys and objects used and "mouthed" by infants
- Changing area washed with bleach solution and dried after each diaper change

b) Uses correct hand washing procedures before and after serving food, diapering/toileting and whenever needed

Examples

- Follows proper handwashing sequence:
    1. wet hands
    2. add liquid soap
    3. wash for twenty seconds
    4. rinse
    5. dry
    6. turn off water using paper towel
- Washes hands thoroughly before and after each diaper change (even when using gloves) and before each feeding
- Washes hands before and after toileting, food preparation, eating, wiping noses and after coming into contact with any bodily fluids

c) Implements sanitary diapering/toileting procedures

Examples

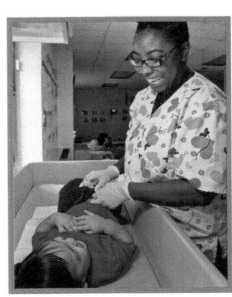

- Follows proper diapering sequence:
    1. organize materials
    2. gently carry child to changing table
    3. clean child's diaper area
    4. remove/dispose of soiled diaper
    5. put on clean diaper and dress child
    6. wash child's hands and return child to supervised area
    7. clean changing table
    8. wash hands and record diaper change in daily log

- Discards soiled disposable diapers in sealed container

- Seals soiled clothes in labeled plastic bags

- Provides extra clothes for children when their clothes become soiled

- Ensures that toilet facilities are sanitary (for example, toilets are flushed after each use, spills of bodily fluids are cleaned with bleach solution)

2.3 Candidate encourages children to practice healthy habits.

a) Ensures that children wash hands properly, with assistance when needed

Examples

- Facilitates children's hand washing and toileting activities in a positive, relaxed and pleasant atmosphere

- Teaches proper hand washing sequence

- Models proper hand washing techniques

- Provides a step stool when necessary so that children can wash hands when they are capable

b) Models, communicates and provides activities that teach the importance of good health to children and families

Examples

- Conducts daily health checks on each child to monitor for symptoms of illness

- Ensures that children wear clothing appropriate for the weather, providing extra clothing as needed

- Recognizes unusual behavior and changes in each child's physical health, encouraging parents to obtain appropriate treatment when needed

- Ensures that children do not share personal items (such as hairbrushes, combs, etc.)

- Enacts procedures for care of sick children (for example, isolates a child with a contagious illness from well children while maintaining supervision, contacts parents and medical providers)

- Uses roleplaying, modeling, visual materials and real objects to teach healthy physical, mental, dental and nutritional practices

- Provides opportunities for toddlers to learn about health care by talking about visits to the doctor and dentist, reading books and encouraging pretend play about health care

- Models how to sneeze into elbow to avoid the spread of germs

- Communicates to children and their parents the importance of outdoor play and physical activity for healthy growth and development

- Recognizes rashes and skin irritations and works with parents to prevent and treat them

- Recognizes the signs of a health crisis that children with special needs may have and responds appropriately (for example, seizures)

- Plans activities that integrate health and nutrition information from the children's cultural groups with medically accepted health and nutrition practices

2.4 Candidate provides appropriate mealtime experiences.

a) Serves nutritious meals and snacks

Examples

- Follows proper storage, preparation and feeding procedures for breast milk

- Follows a sanitary procedure for preparing, storing and labeling baby bottles

- Plans age-appropriate, nutritious menus, meals and snacks that are culturally familiar to children

- Limits sugar, salt, processed foods, unnecessary chemical additives and artificial coloring/flavoring in meals and snacks

- Serves natural, unsweetened fruits, juices and jams/preserves

- Promotes drinking water over sugared drinks

- Includes a variety of fresh fruits and vegetables in meals/snacks

- Ensures that lunches and snacks brought for one child are not shared with other children

- Discusses introduction of new foods to infants/toddlers with families

- Shares nutrition information with families, encouraging them to provide healthy foods when they contribute food to the program

b) Facilitates appropriate mealtime experiences

Examples

- Establishes a relaxed mealtime routine that makes eating pleasant for each child – young infants are held while mobile infants, toddlers feed themselves

- Provides appropriate amounts of food to children

- Encourages children to feed themselves when ready, helping children gradually learn to hold a bottle, drink from a cup, use a utensil and feed themselves

- Respects children's food choices

- Does not require children to finish food on their plates

- Does not use meals/snacks as rewards or punishments

- Holds infants in inclined position during feeding

- Understands and uses the practices that support positive oral development in infants (swabbing gums after feeding, only offering formula/breast milk/water in bottles)

- Adheres to individual feeding schedules

- Does not prop bottles or place bottles in cribs

- Manages group in order to concentrate on the individual feeding of infants

- Does not rush feeding

- Feeds toddlers when hungry

- Facilitates "Family-Style Dining" with toddlers

- Encourages pleasant table conversations with toddlers

- Ensures that toddlers eat while seated rather than when walking, running, playing or lying down

- Offers toddlers opportunities to practice feeding themselves by providing finger foods and following adequate time for pleasurable feeding

- Provides healthy snacks frequently in small portions for toddlers

- Ensures that water is always available for mobile infants and toddlers

Functional Area 3: Learning Environment

Candidate uses space, relationships, materials, and routines as resources for constructing an interesting, secure and enjoyable environment that encourages and fosters trust, play, exploration, interaction and learning.

Item 3.1 Environments are developmentally appropriate for young children.

Indicator:

a) **Environments are pleasant, welcoming and provide appropriate levels of stimulation**

Examples

- Environments are "home-like"

- Bright colors and visual clutter are minimized

- Environments include a variety of natural and pleasurable sounds such as normal conversation, singing, nursery rhymes, outdoor sounds, etc.

- Music is played at a comfortable level and reflects children's cultural groups

- No or few commercial characters are displayed

- Infants are provided with the sights and sounds of other living things — humans, animals and plants — including the Candidate's own face

- Pleasing, culturally-diverse posters or pictures are on display

- Children's art, culturally relevant objects and/or plants/items from nature are present

- A "private" space for toddlers to be on their own or with a friend/caregiver is provided (book corner, cardboard box/barrel, tent, etc.)

b) **Environments are arranged and organized intentionally to meet the developmental needs of children**

Examples

- Environments and materials encourage mouthing, reaching, batting, grasping, babbling and social interaction

- Mobile infants have freedom and opportunities to move and explore in a variety of safe spaces (for example, bare floor, carpet, mattress, grass), protected from older children

- Diapering, toileting and eating areas are separated

- Mobiles are placed over cribs and changing table

- Spaces are designed for appropriate "traffic patterns" for mobile infants and toddlers to move about and participate freely, safely and actively

- For toddlers, spaces and materials are arranged in activity areas for small group or solitary play, pretend play and large muscle climbing equipment/ construction

- Room arrangement encourages participation and interaction of all children, including those with special needs

- Quiet areas (such as the book, art or writing centers) are positioned next to each other, separated from noisier and more active areas (such as blocks or pretend play)

- Environments are designed to help toddlers succeed (for example, block building has enough space and is protected from traffic; areas such as long corridors or large, open spaces that invite children's running or fighting are kept to a minimum)

- Messy activities such as sand/water play and art are located near a source of water for easy cleanup

- Spaces, materials and equipment are provided inside and outside for child-initiated exploration

- Environments are "print-rich," exposing children to the written word at their eye level (such as meaningful signs, labeled shelves and containers, books, etc.)

- Children's art work is displayed respectfully

- Sufficient space is provided for creating and storing completed work and work-in-progress

- A transition area at the entrance of the room provides families with a space to drop off and pick up children and their belongings

- Spaces are adapted as needed for children with special needs

- Space is arranged in identifiable areas that encourage appropriate and independent use of materials

- Spaces provide soft (carpet, pillows, blankets) and hard (vinyl flooring, tables, wooden shelves) surfaces and relaxing furniture (rocking chairs, sofas) that can be enjoyed by both children and adults

- Children are given more space to explore as they become more mobile

3.2 Developmentally appropriate materials are available.

a) Materials are developmentally appropriate for all children, including those with special needs

Examples

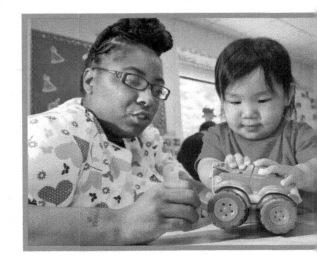

- Materials are engaging, challenging children without being too easy

- Materials demonstrate acceptance of each child's gender, family, race, language, religion and cultural groups

- Easily accessible learning materials are provided that children can explore by themselves (such as puzzles, books, stacking toys)

- Materials are modified to support the needs of all children

b) A variety of materials are provided for children to explore

Examples

- Materials provided include mouthable toys; manipulatives that make noise, can be squeezed, rolled, pushed, pulled; things that move; cause/effect materials; unbreakable mirrors; puzzles; cloth/board books; objects of many textures; sensory materials; puppets

c) There is a sufficient number of materials to accommodate the group size

Examples

- Extra materials are available and rotated into play as children's needs and interests change

- Duplicates of the most popular materials are provided

d) Materials are organized and accessible to children throughout the day

Examples

- Materials are sorted and placed at children's level

- Shelves are labeled with words/pictures

3.3 Daily schedule and weekly plan(s) are developmentally appropriate.

a) Schedule allows for routine needs of children to be met

Examples

- Daily schedule reflects times each day for children's personal needs such as eating/drinking, resting, toileting, etc.

- Rituals for separating from parents are consistently enacted

- Enough time is provided for toddlers to successfully accomplish routine tasks (such as putting on jackets or shoes, participating in clean-up, etc.)

- Consistent routines throughout the day balance active and quiet, free and structured, indoor and outdoor activities

 Candidates seeking Bilingual Specialization must also show evidence of the following:

- A routine for use of the second language in daily activities is established and maintained

b) Schedule provided meets children's needs for play

Example

- Schedules are individualized for infants

- Infants' positions and locations are changed often during the day, responding to each child's developing skills (for example, tummy time, sitting up, rolling over, reaching for objects and making noises)

- Children's changing needs throughout the day - for active play, quiet activity and rest – are planned for and supported

- Children are given time and space for extended, concentrated play

c) Whole group times, when offered, are developmentally appropriate

Examples

- Group Times allow toddlers the choice to participate

- Group Times last as long as toddlers display interest

- Group Times provide many engaging opportunities for active, sensory-oriented learning

d) Weekly plans provide a variety of experiences

Examples

- Weekly plans utilize observational data in order to support goals for both individual and groups of children

- Infants have many individual opportunities each day to interact with the Candidate through eye-to-eye contact and nurturing touch

- Young infants have regular opportunities to go outside to experience various temperatures, light variations, breezes, etc.

- Plans provide a balance of learning experiences: large group, small group, and individualized; child-initiated/led and teacher-initiated/led; active and quiet; structured and unstructured

- Weekly plans include interactions with the community when possible; for example, short trips to local shops, walks around the block, community events

- Plans provide many opportunities for children to interact with each other and the natural world, develop their senses, use their bodies and stimulate their interests

- "Messy" activities, such as water and sand play, finger painting and drawing with markers, are planned

- Process-oriented activities are offered more often than activities intended to create products

- A variety of activities are provided that reflect the cultural groups of the children in the classroom community

 Candidates seeking Bilingual Specialization must also show evidence of the following:

- Uses knowledge of second language development to plan for each child and the group

- Encourages learning in both languages through everyday experiences and activities

- Knows families' views on relevant issues (such as the use of first and second languages within the program, childrearing and biculturalism) and incorporates their views into planning

- Lullabies, songs, games, stories, books and finger plays from both languages are used, asking parents for familiar examples

e) Pleasant nap or quiet times meet children's needs for rest

Examples

- Soothing naptime routines are provided (such as soft music, book-reading or storytelling)

- Warm and responsive caring create an environment of love and trust

- Infants/younger toddlers have individual nap schedules

- Children's backs are gently rubbed

- Toddlers are allowed to hold a security object while resting

- Older toddlers have at least one rest/nap each day for full-day program; quiet time each day for half-day programs

3.4 Candidate's disposition is warm and respectful.

a) Creates a nurturing relationship with each child

Examples

- Smiles often

- Promotes secure attachments by assigning a primary caregiver to each infant

- Frequently carries young infants (in arms or in a sling)

- Responds to young infants' needs for comfort and protection

- Maximizes warm and loving physical contact with young infants by providing a variety of physical contact, from soothing to engaging, depending on the infant's readiness and need

- Makes eye contact with young infants often

- Promptly responds when child communicates by reaching out arms to be picked up, pointing to something of interest, smiling or displaying emotions

- Is upbeat/excited or serious, as appropriate

- Delights in each child's successes

- Expresses kindness and support when a child is having trouble

- Has appropriate physical contact with each child daily in ways that convey love, affection and security

- Uses warm voice, body language and facial expressions with all children

- Talks with and listens to children at their eye level (such as on the floor when reading and at children's table when eating)

- Enjoys children's senses of humor

- Responds immediately and sympathetically to a child's injury or fear of injury, encouraging caring responses by the other children

3.5 Candidate demonstrates sound judgment in using the posted Weekly Schedule/Daily Plan.

a) Generally follows posted schedule and plan

Examples

- Implements daily routines gently and pleasantly, respecting the tempo and sensitivities of each infant or toddler

b) Veers from schedule and plan as needed

Examples

- Embraces "teachable moments" or other learning opportunities when they arise (stays on playground longer when toddlers find a worm or bug of interest, extends time for an activity when children continue to display high interest levels)

- Varies routines spontaneously to take advantage of unusual opportunities (for example, goes outside in the snow, invites a visiting grandmother to share stories or songs, invites the children to watch workers and machinery on the street, plays with one child for an extended amount of time when enough adults are available to care for the group)

- Adapts the daily schedule/plan to accommodate individual children's needs, moods and interests, including children with special needs

- Gives children time to finish activities before transitioning to next activity

- Adjusts activity if not working well

3.6 Candidate effectively facilitates transitional times between activities.

a) Demonstrates an understanding of the importance of transitions

Examples

- Transitions occur in a planned, predictable manner

- Intentionally uses songs, movement, games to engage children's interests or learning throughout each transition (for example, by singing songs, reciting rhymes or poems, counting steps, following the leader's motions, doing movement exercises, etc.)

- Prepares for the next activity so that children do not spend excessive amounts of time waiting

- Alerts toddlers to changes in routine or upcoming transitions well in advance (such as "Five more minutes until Cleanup Time!")

- For those children who have particular difficulty with transitions, gives them an individual warning and explanation of what is to come

- Individualizes transitions from one activity to another with clear directions and patience

- Minimizes the number of transitions between activities

- Minimizes the amount of time children spend in transitions

Competency Standard II:
To advance physical and intellectual competence

Developmental Contexts

Physical:

Young infants *(birth–8 months)* use physical movement, taste, touch, smell, sight, and sound to explore and learn about their world. By moving their arms, hands, legs, and other body parts, by touching and being touched, infants develop an awareness of their bodies and their ability to move and interact with the environment. By using their mouths to explore, hands to reach and grasp, whole bodies to roll over and sit up, they master the necessary strength and skills needed for the developmental stages that follow.

Mobile infants *(9–17 months)* delight in practicing and achieving new physical skills — crawling, standing, sitting down and walking. They interact with their environment in a practical way, using all senses to examine and manipulate objects and begin to understand cause and effect, space, and distance in this way.

Toddlers *(18–36 months)* continue to master physical skills at their own individual rates. Their learning and interaction with the environment continues to be active. Although they are gaining greater control and satisfaction through use of their small muscles (for example, painting, drawing, or working with puzzles), they need opportunities to exercise their large muscles often each day.

Cognitive:

Young infants *(birth–8 months)* learn best within the context of their relationships with caring adults in a secure environment. Some of their early cognitive (intellectual) development includes becoming familiar with distance and space, sounds, similarity and differences among things and visual perspectives from various positions — front, back, under and over.

Mobile infants *(9–17 months)* actively learn through trying things out; using objects as tools; comparing, imitating, looking for lost objects and naming familiar objects, places and people. By giving them opportunities to explore their environment, objects, and people and by sharing children's pleasure in discovery, adults can build children's confidence in their ability to learn and understand.

Toddlers *(18–36 months)* enter into a new and expansive phase of mental activity. They are beginning to think in words and symbols, remember and imagine. Their curiosity leads them to try out materials in many ways and adults can encourage this natural interest by providing a variety of new materials for experimentation. Adults need to create a supportive social environment that contributes to learning by showing enthusiasm for children's individual discoveries and by helping children use words to describe and understand their experiences. Children's cognitive and social development are deeply connected.

Competency Standard II (continued)

Communication:

Young infants *(birth–8 months)* need adults who are attentive to their nonverbal and pre-verbal communication. Adults can provide better care when they respond sensitively to the individual signals of each infant. Infants' early cries, babblings and coos are early forms of communication. Infants' speech development is facilitated by an encouraging partner who responds to their beginning communications and who sings and talks with them about themselves and their world.

Mobile infants *(9–17 months)* begin to babble expressively, name familiar objects and people and understand many words and phrases. Adults can build on this communication by showing an active interest in children's expressions, interpreting their first attempts at words, repeating and expanding on what they say, talking to them clearly, singing songs and telling stories.

Toddlers *(18–36 months)* increase their vocabularies and use of sentences daily. Although there is a wide range of typical language development during this time, it can also be an opportunity for early intervention if there are language delays or difficulties. Adults should communicate actively with all toddlers — model good speech, listen carefully and provide a wide range of vocabulary. Language should be used in a variety of pleasurable ways each day, including songs, stories, instructions, comfort, conversations, information and play.

Creative:

Young and mobile infants *(birth–17 months)* are creative in their individual styles of interacting with the world. Adults can support their creativity by respecting and enjoying the variety of ways very young children express themselves and act on their environment.

Toddlers *(18–36 months)* are interested in using materials to create their own product — sometimes to destroy and create it again or to move on. For example, they become absorbed in dipping a brush in paint and watching their stroke of color on paper. They use their voices and bodies creatively — swaying, chanting and singing. They enjoy making up their own words and rhythms, as well as learning traditional songs and rhymes. Adults can provide water, sand, blocks and other open-ended and raw materials and opportunities for toddlers' creativity and can show respect for what they do. Make-believe and pretend play appear gradually and are signs of emerging cognitive capacity to understand symbols. Adults can join in imaginative play, while helping toddlers distinguish between what is real and what is not.

Functional Area 4: Physical

Candidate uses a variety of developmentally appropriate equipment, learning experiences and teaching strategies to promote the physical development (fine motor and gross motor) of all children.

Item 4.1 Activities, materials and equipment encourage children of varying abilities to develop their large muscles.

Indicator:

a) **Gross motor skills are encouraged through developmentally appropriate materials, equipment and indoor/outdoor activities**

Examples

- Time spent in swings, bouncers, stationary activity centers (exersaucers), high chairs, etc. is limited

- Infants/younger toddlers have safe opportunities to practice creeping, crawling, walking, balancing, climbing, descending stairs, rolling, reaching out, pushing, pulling, standing, throwing, running, etc. both indoors and outdoors

- Platforms, low furniture and ramps are provided so infants and toddlers can explore and pull themselves up

- Older toddlers have safe opportunities to walk, run, climb, jump, throw, kick, dance, gallop, balance, rock, ride, push, pull, pedal, etc.

- Toddlers are provided with materials such as scarves, bean bags, balls, ribbons, as well as containers to fill and dump

- A variety of activities are offered to toddlers that reflect their culture(s), such as dances, music/movement and active games

4.2 Activities and materials encourage children of varying abilities to develop their small muscles.

a) **Individual fine motor skills are encouraged through a variety of developmentally appropriate materials and activities**

Examples

- Appropriate activities and materials are provided to help infants develop fine motor skills such as grasping, dropping, pulling, pushing, throwing, fingering and mouthing

- Infants have opportunities to develop eye-hand coordination in ways that are challenging and satisfying (for example, fitting objects into a hole in a box, self-feeding)

- Infants have opportunities to play with and manipulate a variety of objects

- Mobile infants are encouraged to use a variety of objects and tools (such as pull toys, a pail to carry objects, a shovel to scoop sand, etc.)

- Toddlers have materials appropriate for a range of fine motor skill levels (such as a variety of manipulatives, puzzles with different numbers of pieces, etc.)

- Toddlers have opportunities to use utensils/tools (such as a spoon to stir, a funnel to pour water through, a container to fill and carry objects, a shovel to scoop sand, etc.)

4.3 Activities and materials encourage children to develop their senses.

a) Sight, sound, smell, taste and touch experiences are encouraged through a variety of developmentally appropriate materials and activities

Examples

- Activities offered include opportunities to notice colors, smell scents, distinguish sounds, feel and touch a variety of textures, taste different foods, listen to music from around the world, etc.

- Materials offered include texture boards, smell jars, scented playdough, musical instruments, etc.

- Daily routines are used as opportunities to draw a child's attention to sensory stimuli (such as "the snap on your jacket makes a 'pop' sound," "your orange slice smells delicious," "the water in the table is warm," etc.)

4.4 Candidate's facilitation promotes children's physical development.

a) Participates in physical activities with children, when appropriate

Examples

- Initiates or joins in dancing, game playing, climbing, drawing, painting, etc.

- Ensures that all children are well-supervised before joining in an activity

b) Guides the development of children's fine and gross motor skills

Examples

- Responds positively to each infant's uniquely developing skills (for example, lifting head, sitting up, rolling over, reaching for objects and making noises)

- As children develop, increase the variety and challenge of fine and gross motor activities (for example, introducing ride-on toys, play dough, puzzles, finger plays, equipment for climbing)

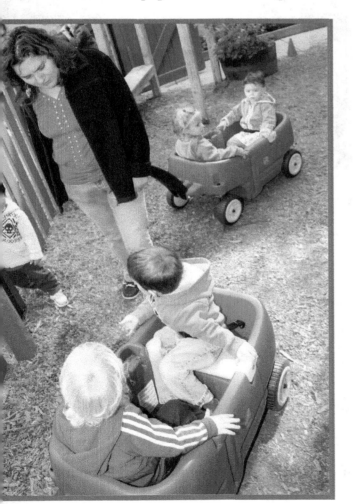

- Offers individualized assistance, learning how children approach and respond to physical challenges

- Encourages children to practice and refine their skills

- Supports and encourages, but does not force, children who are fearful of physical activity

- Offers challenges that will help the child progress without getting frustrated

- Avoids overprotecting children with special needs, supporting their independent functioning and including them in physical activities with other children (making modifications only when necessary)

Functional Area 5: Cognitive

Candidate provides activities and opportunities that encourage curiosity, exploration and problem-solving appropriate to the developmental levels of each child.

Item 5.1 Activities encourage curiosity, exploration and discovery.

Indicator:

a) Activities involve developmentally appropriate, hands-on experiences

Examples

- Infants have many experiences of moving, hiding and changing objects

- Mobile infants and toddlers are provided time for active play and exploration

- Children learn through active experiences

- Engaging activities are meaningful to children's interests

- Activities spark children's natural curiosity

- Experiences provided reflect the range of the children's cultural groups

 Candidates seeking Bilingual Specialization must also show evidence of the following:

- Provides learning experiences that lead to the understanding of basic concepts in the language most familiar to each child

5.2 Materials and equipment stimulate children's thinking and problem-solving.

a) Materials and equipment provide a variety of opportunities for cognitive development

Examples

- Equipment and materials are provided that children can explore and master by themselves

- Infants are provided a variety of objects to inspect and manipulate

- Puzzles, books, manipulatives, water/sand play are provided for toddlers

- Blocks are developmentally appropriate and varied

- Materials and equipment are modified for individual children as needed

b) Materials chosen are meaningful to the children

Examples

- Materials reflect interests expressed by the children

- Materials build on and extend children's interest in the natural world and living things

- Materials reflect children's cultural groups and languages

5.3 Candidate's interactions promote children's thinking and problem solving.

a) Facilitates children's thinking and creative problem-solving skills

Examples

- Listens to children and encourages them to think/talk about what they see, hear, smell, taste and touch

- Models curiosity, inquiry, and investigation for children

- Encourages infants' learning through imitation of others

- Helps toddlers notice cause and effect by providing "if this happens, then that will occur" statements and/or questions

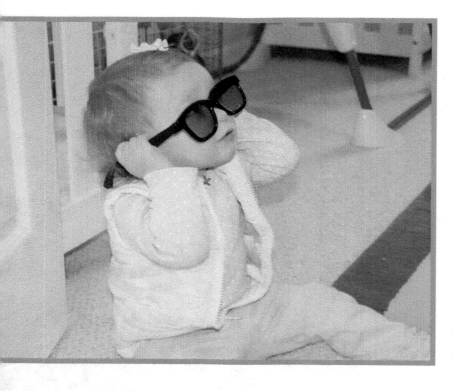

- Encourages toddlers to wonder, guess, and talk about their ideas

- Uses routines such as snack and mealtimes, cleanup, washing hands, dressing for outdoors or rest time as learning opportunities and for children to practice newly acquired skills

- Helps toddlers discover ways to solve problems that arise in daily activities (such as how to put on a jacket, how to walk safely together through the neighborhood, etc.)

- Encourages active learning with toddlers, rather than emphasizing that they listen passively to adults

5.4 Candidate's interactions intentionally build upon children's prior knowledge.

a) Connects concepts to children's previous experiences

Examples

- Listens to infant, imitating sounds and expressions, encouraging a back-and-forth "dialogue"

- Builds on and extends children's knowledge and understanding of their world

- Listens to children and intentionally expands their ideas when appropriate

b) Supports children's repetition of the familiar

Examples

- Supports children's desire to repeat tasks that are familiar them

- Regularly re-reads popular/frequently-requested books

- Provides materials so that children can repeat and practice on their own

Functional Area 6: Communication

Candidate actively communicates with children and provides opportunities and support for children to understand, acquire and to use verbal and nonverbal means of communicating thoughts and feelings.

Item 6.1 Materials promote early literacy.

Indicator:

a) Literacy/storytelling/bookmaking materials are provided

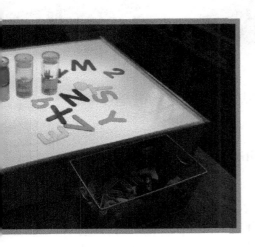

Examples

- Books are attractively displayed on open shelves or in infant-accessible bins, in good condition

- Materials for simple, hand-made infant/toddler books are available (such as Ziploc bags, yarn, cardboard, cloth, etc.)

- Opportunities for verbal expression are provided through puppets, dolls, pretend play clothes/materials, flannel boards, etc.

- Recordings of favorite books/stories are provided for toddlers to listen to (if possible, parents record themselves telling favorite stories and singing songs)

b) Developmentally appropriate books are available

Examples

- Cardboard, vinyl, cloth books, books with textures, patterns, etc. are accessible

- An assortment of books is available including fiction, information books, books related to children's interests, books that reflect the many cultural groups and family structures of the children, books that display non-traditional gender roles, books made by families, tactile books, rhyming books, books with predictable text, books with no words, etc.

- Handmade books with pictures of children's families, pets, friends, etc. are included

- Books in the classroom reflect children's cultural groups, home languages and identities

Candidates seeking Bilingual Specialization must also show evidence of the following:

- Selects books and other appropriate materials in both languages

6.2 Activities promote language development.

a) Children are read to every day

Examples

- Small groups (4 to 6 toddlers) are read to frequently, allowing for greater individual participation, the use of more complex text and engaging conversations about the book

- Children are read books in various languages at different times, but not immediately following the English versions.

b) Activities advance the development of language acquisition and writing skills

Examples

- "Conversations" with infants occur regularly through self-talk and parallel talk, describing Candidate and/or child actions as they occur or are about to occur (for example, "this wipe is a little cold, are you ready?" or "I'm going to pick you up now and take you to the changing table.")

- Writing and reading behaviors are modeled daily as part of normal classroom activities

- Activities include cross-cultural finger plays, games, books, songs used to tell stories; short poems that children enjoy; telling stories without books, dictating stories, etc.

- Activities encourage children to develop listening and comprehension skills (such as telling stories about events that occurred in the children's lives, for example, "Remember when we took a walk to the garden?")

- Toddlers have time to select their own books to look at alone or with a friend(s)

- Toddlers are provided opportunities to use crayons, markers or paintbrushes to help develop fine motor control

- When dual language learners are present, activities help children begin to understand and use the English language while simultaneously developing their primary (home) language

c) Activities provide frequent opportunities for children to listen, talk and express their ideas effectively

Examples

- Infants' sounds and gestures are repeated by the Candidate

- Toddlers are encouraged to notice and imitate sounds in their environment

- Toddlers are encouraged to hear different sounds in the environment (such as, "Can you hear the winds blowing the leaves around the courtyard?")

- Activities encourage toddlers to name objects and talk about their experiences and observations

- Activities allow toddlers to represent their ideas nonverbally (for example, painting, drawing, music-making, dramatic play, puppet play, dance and creative movement)

- Toddlers are encouraged to take turns talking and listening instead of interrupting each other or adults, ensuring that each child has a chance to speak

 Candidates seeking Bilingual Specialization must also show evidence of the following:

- Children have opportunities to express themselves in the language of their choice

d) Activities support the needs of dual language learners (when applicable - see pp. 107-113 for expanded examples)

Examples

- Numerous appropriate experiences help children gain receptive understanding of the new language — specifically, to hear the sounds of the new language and connect them to people, objects and experiences

- Experiences encourage and help children practice sounds and words of the new language, taking into account the stages and patterns of home language and English language acquisition

6.3 Candidate reads to children in a developmentally appropriate manner.

a) Reads to children engagingly

Examples

- Chooses very short picture books to read with infants

- Props up books for infants to see

- Infants and toddlers may pat, touch, point to and name pictures in books

- Holds book so that all children can see pictures during reading

- Keeps children's attention by holding eye contact, speaking clearly, matching tempo with the book's story, "acting out" the book using character voices, hand/body movements, facial expressions, etc.

6.4 Candidate's interactions encourage children's communication skills.

a) Promotes children's language development through her/his verbal and non-verbal communications

Examples

- Has realistic expectations for each child's understanding and use of speech based on knowledge of language development and the individual child

- Reads and sings to infants

- Names objects for infants

- Uses gestures to demonstrate the meaning of words to infants

- Uses everyday routines (such as diapering and feeding) as opportunities for talking with and listening to infants

- Responds to children's crying as a form of communication

- Talks with children about their experiences and home lives

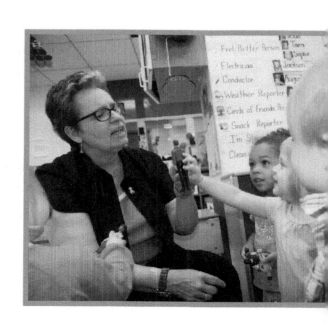

- Does not dominate conversations; talks only as long as children are interested

- Takes turns when talking with child; talks with, not at, child

- Elaborates on toddlers' short phrases to help them express intended meaning ("Milk? You want more milk?")

- Models standard grammatical speech

- Models and encourages children's creativity in language; for example, through rhymes, imaginative stories and nonsense words

- Uses varied, attention-grabbing, affectionate and playful tones when appropriate

- Communicates, with eyes and voice, attention and interest to an exploring child at a distance from the caregiver

- Reads and sings to toddlers frequently both individually or in groups of 2 or 3 in close physical contact

- Shows delight with sounds/words/gestures child makes

 Candidates seeking Bilingual Specialization must also show evidence of the following:

- Demonstrates ability to understand, speak, read and write both languages

- Helps children feel good about themselves as speakers of each language

- Supports the child's attempt to use either language

b) Interacts with children, listening and responding appropriately

Examples

- Imitates cooing and babbling, making eye contact, encouraging a "conversation" led by the infant

- Responds to infant's body signs and nonverbal cues that signal discomfort, excitement, pleasure, etc., and verbally describes the infant's experience

- Listens carefully to an infant's cry and responds quickly and appropriately: allows an infant to cry briefly when settling into sleep, comforts an infant who is distressed and feeds an infant who is hungry

- Recognizes and responds to emotional cues, social gestures and sounds of infants, elaborating appropriately

- Talks to each child frequently about her/his family — where they are, when they will come back, and what they do together

- Listens attentively to children, tries to understand what they want to communicate, and helps them to express themselves

- Listens to toddlers with respect, giving them enough time to respond to a question or comment

- Accepts toddlers' grammar without correcting

c) Supports the needs of dual language learners (when applicable - see pp. 107-113 for expanded examples)

Examples

- Is knowledgeable about and respectful of each child's family, cultural groups and home languages

- Establishes responsive and accepting relationships to help children feel confident to engage in receptive and verbal communication in either language (home language or new language)

6.5 Candidate promotes children's vocabulary development

a) Intentionally provides opportunities for children to learn new words

Examples

- Labels or names objects and events to help children learn new words

- Uses "Parallel talk" to facilitate infants' learning (for example, talks to infants, describing what

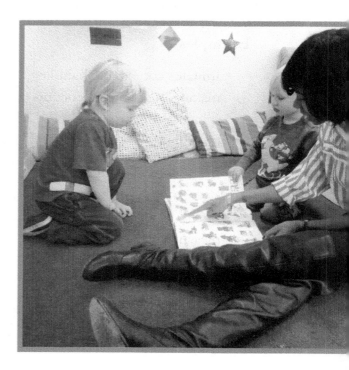

they feel, hear, touch, smell, see or, for referencing cause and effect, saying "When you pushed the ball, it rolled away")

- Names and talks about infants' feelings, clothing, body parts, etc.

- Explains words using synonyms and antonyms

- Helps infants and toddlers connect word meaning(s) to experiences and real objects (for example, acknowledges crying infant and tells him, "Let's change your diaper," patting his diaper to reinforce the message and the term "diaper")

- Looks at and talks enthusiastically about picture books with toddlers

 Candidates seeking Bilingual Specialization must also show evidence of the following:

- Provides opportunities for all children to acquire a second language

- Helps children associate word meanings in both languages with familiar objects and experiences

- Takes an active role in labeling children's actions and surroundings in their home language, encouraging children's use of these words

b) Regularly introduces children to more advanced vocabulary

Examples

- Names and talks about infants' feelings, behaviors, activities, clothing, body parts, introducing new words whenever possible

- Regularly introduces more complex vocabulary into conversations with toddlers (for example, rather than describing a block tower as "big," says, "That tower is gigantic; it's really big!")

- Responds to toddlers' speech with expansions and questions, introducing and explaining new words

- Does not correct toddlers' grammatical speech errors. Instead, restates them correctly. (For example, a toddler may say, "I gots two foots" and the teacher replies, "Yes, you have two feet so you need two socks.")

Functional Area 7: Creative

Candidate provides opportunities that encourage children to play with sound, rhythm, language, materials, space and ideas in individual ways and to express their creative abilities.

Item 7.1 Activities and materials encourage children to express themselves through the visual arts.

Indicator:

a) Art materials and activities are available for children daily

Examples

- Open-ended drawing/coloring materials are available rather than coloring books/sheets

- Activities that focus on processes are offered rather than activities intended only to create certain products

- Infants and toddlers are provided large sheets of plain paper, fat crayons, wide water color markers or other creative tools/materials

- Toddlers are provided many colors of construction paper, water color markers, safety scissors, glue, glue sticks, stamp pads, tempera/watercolor paints, collage materials, play dough or clay, chalk, paints, a variety of papers, brushes or other art tools/materials

- Art activities, materials and techniques are offered that reflect the cultural groups of the classroom community

7.2 Activities and materials encourage children to dance, move and develop their musical abilities.

a) Music and dance/movement materials and activities are available for children daily

Examples

- Infants are held by Candidate as they "dance" together

- Mobile infants and toddlers do fingerplays, sing, dance and move creatively

- Toddlers and Candidate make up songs and music together

- Toddlers play with games with music/musical instruments

- Children regularly hear a variety of musical forms and styles

- Children are offered activities that explore rhythm

- Materials for free or organized play include musical sound toys, ribbons, scarves and musical instruments (such as drums, bells, triangles, wood blocks and tambourines)

- Music and dance activities are offered that reflect the cultural groups of the classroom community

7.3 Activities and materials encourage children to develop their imaginations.

a) Dramatic play materials and activities are available for children daily

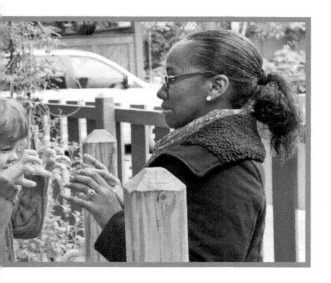

Examples

- A variety of dress-up clothes are available for toddlers (gender-specific and non-specific clothing, uniforms, costumes, etc.)

- A variety of dramatic play props (such as dolls, blankets, mirrors, purses, telephones, briefcases, a dollhouse, small people/animal figures, puppets, puppet stage, etc.)

- Dramatic play activities and materials are offered that reflect the cultural groups of the classroom community

7.4 Candidate promotes individual expression and creativity.

a) Encourages creative self-expression in children's activities

Examples

- Is alert and responsive to infants' initiatives to play, move, and use materials, gradually introducing new things to be combined and used in ways that infants can invent; for example, pieces of fabric of different colors and textures, rhythm instruments or objects that make different noises, assorted empty food containers.

- In the visual arts, values toddlers' "scribble" pictures, does not expect them to look like others

- In music & dance, encourages children to move in their own ways, make their own music and songs

- In dramatic play, encourages children to pretend in their own ways

- Participates in dramatic play to get it going if toddlers have difficulty, or to extend it (such as, entering the play restaurant and pretending to be a customer, "Could I see a menu, please? I'd like to order dinner.")

- Models creativity (for example, displays her own artwork, reads children a poem she wrote or plays a guitar with children)

- Keeps informed about cultural resources in the community and uses them with children when possible

 Candidates seeking Bilingual Specialization must also show evidence of the following:

- Helps children express themselves creatively through activities in both languages

b) Facilitates child-directed and process-oriented creative experiences

Examples

- Plans activities that are not designed to result in identical finished products

- Allows toddlers to create abstract art; not expecting them to always create representational products

- Does not present a model for a finished product

- Gradually introduces different art materials, giving children time to explore them in their own ways, showing interest in their process

- Encourages children to explore textures, colors and the sensory experiences of materials

- Offers the option to record children's descriptions of their work

- In dramatic play, follows the toddler's lead, taking care not to over-stimulate or frighten the child

- Accepts/encourages flexible use of materials when possible (such as allowing children to carry pretend animals from the Science Area to the Sand Table or paint with a feather at an easel)

Competency Standard III:

To support social and emotional development and to provide positive guidance

Developmental Contexts

Self:

Young infants *(birth–8 months)*, during the first few weeks and months, begin to build a sense of self-confidence and security in an environment where they can trust that an adult will lovingly care for their needs. Infants are only emerging in their ability to regulate their temperature and recognize signs of discomfort such as hunger or feeling cold. An adult who cares for a young infant provides immense support for future abilities in self regulation by being consistently available. The adult feeds the child when hungry, keeps the child warm and comfortable, soothes the child when distressed and offers learning opportunities by providing interesting things to look at, taste, smell, feel, hear and touch.

Mobile infants *(9–17 months)*, a loving caregiver is a resource or "home base" who is readily available and provides warm physical comfort and a safe environment to explore and master. This emotional stability is essential for the development of self-confidence as well as language, physical, cognitive and social growth.

Toddlers' *(18–36 months)* sense of self and growing feelings of independence develop at the same time that they realize the importance of parents and other caregivers. The healthy toddler's inner world is filled with conflicting feelings and ideas — independence and dependence, confidence and doubt, fear and curiosity, hostility and love, anger and tenderness, aggression and passivity. Understanding the wide range of toddlers' feelings and how they might be expressed can help support the adult's ability to provide a calm and emotionally secure environment.

Social:

Young infants *(birth–8 months)* enter the world with an innate capacity and need for social contact. Yet each baby is unique in styles of interacting and readiness for different kinds of interactions. Infants need both protective and engaging social interactions with a few consistent, caring adults who get to know them as individuals. When adults respond to the cues and signals of young infants, they model social interactions. It is through these early experiences that babies learn to read and respond appropriately to the cues of others.

Mobile infants *(9–17 months)* are curious about others but need assistance and supervision in interacting with other children. They continue to need one or a few consistent adults as their most important social partner(s) and as a bridge to creating additional social partners.

Competency Standard III (continued)

Toddlers *(18–36 months)* social awareness is much more complex than that of younger children. Toddlers can begin to understand that others have feelings too — sometimes similar to and sometimes different from their own. They imitate many of the social behaviors of other children and adults. As toddlers become increasingly interested in other children, adults should guide and support their interactions, recognizing that they continue to rely upon familiar adults for emotional stability.

Guidance:

Young infants *(birth–8 months)* begin to adapt their rhythms of eating and sleeping to the expectations of their social environment through the gentle guidance of sensitive caregivers who meet their needs. Infants basic trust in adults and their environment that is established at this time directly affects the child's responsiveness to positive guidance later and promotes the development of self-regulation.

Mobile infants *(9–17 months)* want to do everything but they have little understanding about what is permissible and may not remember rules. Adults can organize the environment in ways that clearly define limits and minimize conflicts. While respecting the child's experiments by saying "no," they can reinforce positive social interaction (for example, hugging) and discourage negative behaviors (for example, biting).

Toddlers *(18–36 months)* move through recurring phases of extreme dependence and independence as they gain new skills and awareness. They require an understanding caregiver who remains calm and supportive during their struggle to become independent. Adults must be resourceful in recognizing and encouraging self-regulatory behavior while setting consistent, clear limits.

Functional Area 8: Self

Candidate develops a warm, positive, supportive and responsive relationship with each child and helps each child learn about and take pride in his or her individual and cultural identities.

Item 8.1 Children's environments support the development of positive self-concepts.

Indicator:

a) Spaces and activities help each child develop a sense of self-identity/worth

Examples

- Spaces are set up so that infants and toddlers can practice self-help skills

- Toddlers have spaces to store their own things (such as cubbies/hooks/bins labeled with children's names and/or photos)

- Toddler's books, pictures, stories and discussions help children identify with the events and experiences of their lives (for example, single-parent families, extended families, same-sex families, adoption, foster families, divorce, moving, birth of siblings, or death of family members or beloved pets)

- Photos of children and families are displayed throughout

- Children's works and names are displayed respectfully

- Mirrors are hung at children's eye level

- Each child's developing awareness of him/herself as a member of a family and of an ethnic or social group is supported through conversations about families (using photographs, mirrors or other appropriate objects) and by celebrating relevant cultural events with children

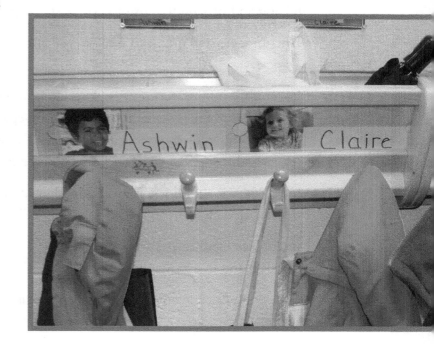

- All children, including those with special needs, are provided activities that support them in feeling effective and experiencing success

b) Materials chosen provide children opportunities to experience success

Examples

- Materials selected provide developmentally appropriate challenges that each child can accomplish

- Over time, materials are changed to provide greater challenges as children develop

- Materials are modified so that all children, including those with special needs, may experience success

8.2 Candidate's interactions help children develop positive self-concepts.

a) Respects the individuality of each child

Examples

- Knows and uses each child's preferred name

- Creates a personal relationship with each infant, knowing the kind of cuddling, stroking, talking and playing that brings comfort and positive feelings to each individual infant

- Encourages each infant to grab an object of choice

- For mobile infants, recognizes typical periods of development when the child has difficulty separating from family members or is fearful of new adults and is supportive of the child and the family

- Uses everyday routines to give individual attention to each child

- Recognizes and respects each child's physical and emotional boundaries

- Gives one-on-one attention to each child as much as possible

- Encourages children to try new and different activities

- Allows each child to work at her/his own pace and in his/her style

- Encourages children to choose any activity free of its traditionally gender-specific association

- Supports the individual independence of children with special needs, including them in physical and social activities with other children (making modifications when necessary)

- Is able to speak some words in a child's home language (when applicable)

 Candidates seeking Bilingual Specialization must also show evidence of the following:

- Helps each child deal with stressors using the child's first language

b) Shows sensitivity to and acceptance of each child's feelings and needs

Examples

- Talks with infants about their feelings

- Does not startle an infant (for example, picks up infant from front not back, explaining what is happening)

- Changes infants' positions and locations often during the day

- Uses words to describe toddler's feelings

- Welcomes a child who needs to be nurtured with a loving voice, hugging or appropriate physical contact

- Responds to children's feelings (such as love, joy, loneliness, anger or disappointment) with sympathetic/empathetic attention.

- Responds immediately and sympathetically to a child's injury or fear of injury

- Quickly comforts children who are upset

- Helps children understand and appropriately express their own feelings.

- Respects children's preferences

- Is patient with each child

- Focuses on each child's positive qualities rather than comparing them with each other

- Helps children through periods of stress, separation, life transitions and other crises

- Does not criticize children's efforts

- Understands the effect of abuse and neglect on children's self-concept and works sensitively with such children

- Celebrates children's cultural identities

- Helps children recognize, accept and express feelings in culturally appropriate ways

8.3 Candidate encourages children to develop a sense of independence.

a) Encourages children's self-help/self-regulation skills while being respectful of family preferences and cultural differences

Examples

- Understands and respects the individual eating and sleeping needs of healthy infants and responds to infants in ways that support emerging regulation skills

- Helps each infant begin to self-regulate into regular sleeping/eating patterns by providing support to assist infant in soothing/calming herself

- Makes routines like feeding/eating, toileting, dressing opportunities for toddlers to acquire self-help skills, begin to regulate their behavior and learn language

- Encourages children to feed themselves when ready

- Supports toddlers' growing toileting skills

- Helps toddlers to develop self- help skills in eating, washing hands, cleaning up their own spills etc.

• Provides opportunities for toddlers to learn to help themselves (for example, taking off jackets or pouring milk) and shares children's pleasure in acquiring new skills

b) Ensures that toileting is a developmentally appropriate, positive experience for children

Examples

• Encourages toilet learning when each toddler is ready and interested

• Encourages toddlers to use the toilet by themselves

• Shows toddlers how to use good toilet habits (such as wiping properly, lifting and lowering seat and aiming well)

• Does not shame or rush children

• Does not reward or punish children for toileting behaviors

• Works with parents in planning for toilet learning, respecting different family practices

c) Promotes each child's growing sense of autonomy

Examples

• Offers finger foods to older infants

• Encourages toddlers to use utensils

• Provides a step stool when needed so that toddlers can use the toilet and wash their hands when they are capable

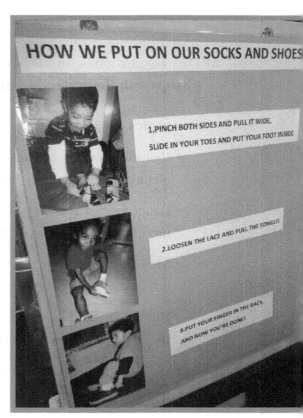

HOW WE PUT ON OUR SOCKS AND SHOES

1. PINCH BOTH SIDES AND PULL IT WIDE, SLIDE IN YOUR TOES AND PUT YOUR FOOT INSIDE

2. LOOSEN THE LACE AND PULL THE TONGUE

3. PUT YOUR FINGER IN THE BACK, AND NOW YOU'RE DONE!

Functional Area 9: Social

Candidate helps each child feel accepted in the group, helps children learn to communicate and get along with others and encourages feelings of empathy and mutual respect among children and adults.

Item 9.1 The classroom environment provides opportunities for children to practice cooperation.

Indicator:

a) Materials, equipment and activities provided help children experience working and playing in harmony

Examples

- Children participate in some activities in small groups

- Some manipulatives, materials or equipment invite cooperation between toddlers

- Multiple copies of "popular" items are provided to reduce fighting among mobile infants and toddlers

9.2 A non-biased environment is provided.

a) Diverse activities, materials, curricula and/or events reflect multiple cultural groups, ethnicities and family structures

Examples

- Pictures, posters, books, and other materials reflect and celebrate diversity in cultural groups, ages, genders, differing abilities and varied family structures

- Languages, real objects, music, art, foods and many aspects of cultural groups are incorporated into the curriculum

- Members of the local community are invited to share aspects their lives (such as hobbies, cooking, talents, holidays, dress, etc.) with the toddlers

- Props associated with special needs and diverse cultural groups are included throughout the toddler classroom

- Holidays/events are celebrated that reflect the diverse families of the classroom community

Candidates seeking Bilingual Specialization must also show evidence of the following:

- Uses objects, music activities and celebrations that are meaningful to young children to encourage development of both languages and cultural groups

9.3 Candidate promotes children's sense of belonging in the classroom community.

a) Encourages children's social interactions

Examples

- Takes advantage of opportunities for social play during feeding, changing, dressing and other daily routines

- Provides infants with opportunities to observe social interactions between older children and among adults

- Creates opportunities for social interactions among mobile infants/toddlers, remaining available to protect, comfort or facilitate, not interfering unless necessary

- Facilitates developmentally appropriate interactions between toddlers (such as consistently acknowledging toddlers' pro-social behaviors and not reacting negatively when a toddler is unable to share or wait to take a turn)

- Acknowledges when infants and toddlers act with caring and compassion towards others

- Provides many opportunities for toddlers to interact and play with each other

- Introduces toddlers to the idea of respecting the rights and possessions of others

- Encourages toddlers to share but never blames them if they are not yet capable

- Encourages children to comfort and help one another

- Acknowledges children's caring or helpful behaviors

- Understands that the social roles and expectations for children in their family setting may be different from those of the child care program, helping the children successfully socialize in both settings

- Helps children, including those shy and aggressive, to get along with others

- Ensures positive integration of all children including those with special needs (when applicable)

 Candidates seeking Bilingual Specialization must also show evidence of the following:

- Understands that the social roles and expectations for bilingual children in their family setting may be different from those of the child care program, helping the children successfully socialize in both settings

b) Models appropriate social interactions

Examples

- Provides infants with opportunities to observe social interactions between older children and among adults

- Models effective social skills by building a positive relationship with each child, parent and other adults in the center

- Models social skills by engaging in social interactions with children (such as conversing with children at mealtime or while putting toys away)

- Warmly introduces newcomers

- Models for and teaches toddlers skills that help them learn how to join in, start and sustain play with others

- Models and encourages toddlers to ask for, accept and give help to one another

- Models and participates in dialogues or conversations with children

9.4 Candidate helps children experience sympathy/empathy and respect for others.

a) Helps children understand their feelings and the feelings of others

Examples

- Helps children recognize their own and others' feelings, similarities and differences in order to help them begin learning how to empathize with others

- Talks with a child about another child's feelings

- Labels children's feelings and the feelings of others (such as "Vincent seems sad because his mommy left. Do you remember how you felt when your mom left this morning?")

- Acknowledges children's developing empathetic responses to one another and adults

- Encourages children to express how they feel

- Models empathy

- Helps children to see how what they do affects others

- Helps toddlers understand that sometimes they must wait for attention because of other children's needs

b) Discusses diversity comfortably when interacting with children

Examples

- Uses children's individual differences as opportunities for learning about how people are alike and different

- Understands toddlers' explorations, curiosities and concerns about their own and others' bodies, responding with developmentally appropriate information (such as explaining the physical differences between boys and girls matter-of-factly, in simple terms)

- Helps children recognize and appreciate racial, ethnic and ability differences and similarities

- Encourages play and relationships among all children across racial, language, ethnic, age, and gender groupings, including children with special needs

- Models equitable treatment of all children and families

Functional Area 10: Guidance

Candidate provides a supportive environment and uses effective strategies to help all children learn and practice appropriate and acceptable behaviors as individuals and as a group, and effectively provides support for children with persistent challenging behaviors.

Item 10.1 Spaces and materials are arranged to promote positive interactions and limit disruptive behaviors.

Indicator:

a) Spaces and materials provided anticipate children's behavioral and developmental needs

Examples

- Ample space is provided for groups of mobile infants or toddlers to move and play

- Equipment is available for children who need to move

- Multiple copies of popular toys are provided to minimize conflicts and waiting

- Furniture is arranged to reduce or eliminate problem behaviors (such as running, etc.)

- Space that feels private (but is well-supervised) is provided for toddlers who need time to be alone

10.2 Candidate proactively implements methods for preventing behavioral problems.

a) Acknowledges positive behaviors

Examples

- Notices self-regulation and kind behaviors, verbally or non-verbally

- Ignores minor distractions

- Tells children what they can do rather than what they cannot do

- Comments directly, sincerely and positively to children about their performance and ideas

- Does not use stickers or other rewards

b) Models appropriate behaviors

Examples

- Models sharing, taking turns, waiting

- Models social problem-solving (how to resolve a conflict with someone else)

- Models appropriate ways for children to behave (such as using an "inside" voice)

c) Provides firm, consistent limits and expectations

Examples

- Helps children under-stand that kind, co-operative behavior is expected

- Gives positively worded directions (such as "Give gentle touches" rather than "Don't hit")

- Establishes guidelines for toddlers' behavior that are simple, reasonable, and consistent

 Candidates seeking Bilingual Specialization must also show evidence of the following:

- Uses clear and simple words in both languages to describe limits and expectations

d) Uses effective classroom management techniques

Examples

- Gently provides guidance to the exploring infant who is frustrated by an obstacle, comforts the child, and provides either strategies or an alternative activity

- Understands that sharing, taking turns, and playing with others is difficult for toddlers and encourages their attempts to use words to resolve conflicts

- Recognizes toddlers' "oppositional" behaviors (saying "no," tantrums, etc.) as part of typical development

- Moves about room as children play, talking with and helping them, encouraging children to participate

- Is aware of each child's limitations, temperament, developmental levels, cultural groups, etc. and individualizes guidance accordingly

- Explains rules at the child's level of understanding

- Gives children acceptable choices when appropriate and follows what each child chooses (for example, "Do you want to read a book with me or play on the climber?" or "Should we have apples or bananas for snack today?")

- Is able to modify play when it becomes overstimulating for any of the children, including children with special needs or sensitive temperaments

- Anticipates confrontations between children and defuses provocative behaviors

- Makes sure there is enough room at the table or play area so children are not crowded

- Reinforces positive behaviors

- Anticipates and prevents the escalation of confrontations between children.

- Addresses the problem behavior or situation rather than labeling the child involved

- Explains the reasons for limits in simple words, demonstrating whenever possible

- Anticipates and responds to children's behaviors, knowing each child's individual differences/tendencies to bite, pinch, climb, escape, etc.

e) Helps children learn to articulate their emotions and practice how to respond in challenging situations

Examples

- Helps toddlers learn how to use words rather than actions to resolve conflicts

- Supports children in finding alternate behaviors that meet their needs when undesirable but developmentally expected social behaviors occur (such as biting, hitting, spitting, etc.)

- Accepts and helps children accept "negative" feelings and find safe ways to deal with them

- Provides activities such as throwing foam balls, bean bags, manipulating playdough to children who need to release negative feelings peacefully

10.3 Candidate uses positive techniques when reacting to children's challenging behaviors.

a) Places emphasis on the development of self-discipline/self-regulation

Examples

- Uses gentle reminders when rules are momentarily forgotten or not followed

- Introduces toddlers to positive alternatives to socially unacceptable behavior (such as teaching a child to "use your words" rather than grabbing a toy from another child)

b) Deals with challenging behaviors in a consistent and calm manner

Examples

- Assesses challenging behaviors or conflicts as they arise, intervening when appropriate

- Uses a range of effective strategies to individualize each child's guidance

- Responds consistently over time to each child's behavioral problems

- Responds quickly and calmly to prevent children from hurting each other

- Is fair and firm if "no" must be said

- Avoids power struggles

- Maintains calm self-control when dealing with an aggressive child

• Communicates with children effectively when behavioral issues arise (such as positioning at their eye level, speaking softly/privately, using positive but serious facial expressions/body language, etc.)

c) Uses appropriate techniques to address negative behaviors

Examples

- Is aware of own bias towards what is fair or just and is able to moderate those beliefs based on developmental information of the child (for example, a toddler takes a toy away from a baby, but the baby does not react and just picks up another toy — the Candidate realizes that this action does not need adult intervention)

- Uses redirection, providing children with a variety of positive options, stating clearly what children can do

- Uses firm "no" only when necessary to maintain children's safety, moving the child or dangerous object, giving a simple explanation (for example, "It is not safe for you to climb on the table. I don't want you to fall and get hurt.")

- When responding to tantrums, isolates and stays close to the child when she/he may hurt or do damage, letting the other children know that "she is having a difficult moment and I am helping her stay safe."

- Does not use negative disciplinary methods (such as spanking, threatening, shouting, isolating, shaming or time-outs)

Competency Standard IV:
To establish positive and productive relationships with families

Developmental Context

Families:

Young infants *(birth–8 months)* are establishing patterns of sleeping, waking, eating, playing, and social activity. They can be supported in developing some stability in these routines by the sensitive and consistent responses of adults. Families and caregivers can anticipate needs and respond more appropriately to the infant's signals when they share details with each other about the baby at drop off and pick up times.

Mobile infants *(9–17 months)* may have difficulty separating from the family members even when the caregiver is a familiar and trusted person. Caregivers can support infants and their families by recognizing that it may be upsetting both for the adults and the child and providing strategies to ease the separation. Caregivers should recognize the potential for competition between themselves and parents and work to avoid it, remembering that babies can have more than one important adult in their lives. Caregivers and families also need to agree on reasonable and safe limits as children begin to explore and wander.

Toddlers *(18–36 months)* develop their own special routines and rituals in order to feel safe and secure. It is essential that families and caregivers share their experiences and understanding of the child's patterns and provide consistent, dependable support for the toddler's developing sense of self competence and confidence.

Functional Area 11: Families

Candidate establishes a positive, responsive, cooperative relationship with each child's family, engages in two-way communication with families, encourages their involvement in the program and supports the child's relationship with her/his family.

Item 11.1 Various opportunities to appreciate and communicate with children's families are included as part of the regular program.

Indicator:

a) Room displays and materials reflect respect for various communities, cultural groups and families

Examples

- Photos/posters of diverse children and their families are displayed at children's eye level

- Books/albums with pictures of children, their families and their communities are accessible to children

 Candidates seeking Bilingual Specialization must also show evidence of the following:

- Environment clearly communicates to families that their home language is valued and respected

b) Opportunities to communicate with and distribute information to families are provided

Examples

- Parents of infants receive daily reports about their child's eating, sleeping and diaper changes

- Family Board ensures that families have access to current information about the program

- Each child/family has a designated container for classroom or program "mail," artwork, writing samples, etc. (such as pouches, folders, bins)

- Regular (daily, weekly) communications are sent home that provide families with information about current/upcoming events, classroom needs, etc. (such as newsletters, blogs, emails, texts or through a regularly-updated website)

11.2 Candidate appreciates the uniqueness of each family.

a) Welcomes and respects every family

Examples

- Knows family members and greets them by name

- Appropriately uses information about each child's family in conversations, program activities, conferences and throughout the curriculum

- Recognizes that parents and family are the most important people in children's lives, making sure to never create a sense of competition

- Welcomes and encourages family members to visit throughout the day

- Helps parents with separations from child, recognizing parents' possible concerns about leaving their child

- Invites families to take part in program activities

- Honors each family's dietary, dress or other preferences for their children

- Respects families' views when they differ from the program's goals or policies and attempts to resolve the differences

- Recognizes that children's primary caregivers may be single mothers or fathers, two parents of the same or different genders, stepparents, grandparents, uncles, aunts, sisters, brothers, foster parents, or guardians

- Respects each family's cultural background, religious beliefs, and childrearing practices, negotiating openly any areas of discomfort or concern

 Candidates seeking Bilingual Specialization must also show evidence of the following:

- Greets visitors using salutations in both languages

11.3 Candidate partners with families to support the needs of their children.

a) Works closely with each family

Examples

- Works with families to understand meaning of baby's cries and to respond sensitively

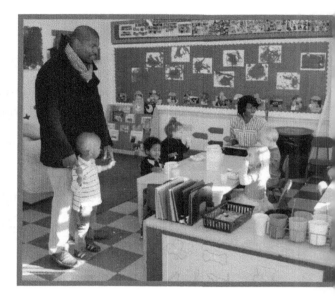

- Coordinates toilet learning plans with family and frequently communicates on child's progress

- Encourages families to share their views about childrearing, guidance and self-regulation

- Builds a trusting relationship with children and families

- Helps families understand their child's temperament, providing and soliciting further ideas and suggestions for support

- Supports and encourages families in becoming observers of their children

- Helps families cope with and plan for supportive transitions into and out of the program as well as from room to room.

- Gives families an integral role in establishing goals for their children's learning and development

- Encourages and assists parents to communicate confidently about their children with government and other community agencies

- Collaborates with families to plan program events and topics for discussion

b) Maintains open communication with families

Examples

- Communicates frequently with parents about children's health, nutrition, communicable diseases and medications

- Sends home written observations and explanations of what children learned, experienced and achieved

- Encourages families to share observations, anecdotes and perspectives about their child.

- Is able to discuss learning challenges or problem behaviors with families in a constructive, supportive manner

- Shares with families her/his pleasure in each child's new abilities

- Shares children's achievements with parents (such as communication/language, physical, social, cognitive, etc.)

- Discusses problem behaviors with families in a strengths-based, constructive, supportive manner

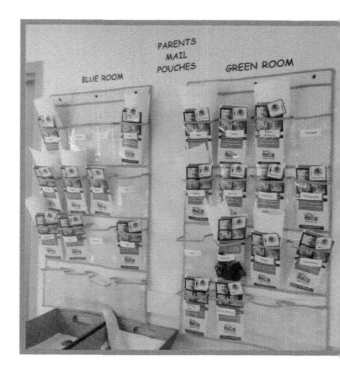

- Regularly holds conferences during which teachers and families can share information about children's progress at home and in the program.

- Conducts home visits or if parents prefer, meets privately with them at a comfortable site (such as a library or local community center)

- Shows sincere interest in what families share and exchanges information regularly with parents about the child's life at home and in the center, including routines and changes in care, favorite activities, upcoming developmental expectations, etc.

- Provides oral and written communication with parents in their preferred language

- Respects the language of non-English-speaking families, encouraging them to communicate freely with their children in their preferred language and helping them find opportunities to learn English

- Is careful not to overshadow parents' natural desire to be the ones who discover their child's first milestones (for example, if a child takes his first step, tells the parent that the child "tried to walk today")

Candidates seeking Bilingual Specialization must also show evidence of the following:

- Regularly communicates orally and in writing with parents and children in their preferred language

- Provides written information for families in both languages (such as classroom newsletters, notices about immunizations, program policies, notices of upcoming events, etc.)

11.4 Candidate helps families understand and support the healthy growth and development of their child.

a) Provides information and opportunities to help families meet their child's developmental needs

Examples

- Talks with parents about the meaning of an infant's beginning communications (for example, different kinds of crying)

- Responds with interest and information to concerns of families about sleep, waking, feeding, or other issues related to infant's needs and development

- Shares information with families concerning nutrition, including appropriate ages for weaning and introducing solid foods, while showing respect for different family practices and values

- Provides information to parents about providing a safe home environment as infants become more and more mobile

- Helps families understand a mobile infant's possible fear of strangers

- Converses with parents of mobile infants about emerging independence and the child's use of the word "no."

- Discusses with families the developmental reasons for toddlers' emotional outbursts and negative behaviors, offering suggestions for handling them based on what works in the classroom, asking families to share the strategies that work for them at home

- Helps families understand the importance of play for children

- Sends home articles, brochures on various topics related to child development

- Offers a parent resource library of books, magazines, journals, DVDs, etc.

- Provides a website with links to various parenting and child development resources

- Empathizes with families around stressful areas of parenting, such as lack of sleep, illnesses, challenging behaviors, providing support and suggestions for strategies when asked

- Shares realistic expectations with families about children's behaviors in ways that help avoid disciplinary problems (for example, discussing how long children can sit still or that toddlers cannot yet follow multiple step directions)

- Provides parent education events with local speakers

- Invites parents to observe the children and discuss their observations

- Helps parents recognize their feelings and attitudes about special needs

 Candidates seeking Bilingual Specialization must also show evidence of the following:

- Understands the principles and characteristics of bilingual language development in children and explains these to parents

- Helps families understand the importance of children learning their primary language and cultural group

- Helps families understand the program goals for bilingual development

- Explains to families in their second language safety practices used in the classroom

- Regularly communicates with parents about their child's bilingual development and helps them find ways to support this within the family

- Supports families' desire to communicate their language and cultural heritage to their children

- If using translated material, ensures the information is as relevant and accurate as the original provided in English.

b) Knows the social service, health and education resources of the community, engaging them when appropriate

Examples

- Helps families find resources about possible impairments or delays that affect hearing and speech

- Observes and evaluates children's physical development, recognizing signs of possible physical disabilities and developmental delays, referring parents to appropriate services, and following up on referrals or individual development plans

- Recognizes that sometimes serious behavior problems are related to developmental or emotional problems and works cooperatively with parents and other professionals towards solutions

- Works with family members and specialists to develop plans specific to the needs of each child and works with the family to meet goals for the child

- Establishes relationships (through a liaison) with community services that respond to family violence (such as Parents Anonymous, Child Protective Services and local shelter programs)

- Works as part of a team to help identify, diagnose, and implement individualized plans for children with special needs

- Shares with families clear and understandable information about their children's special needs and information about the family's legal right to services

- Informs families about resources (such as physicians or community clinics) which provide services to families in their primary language

- Provides information about local language translation services, as needed

 Candidates seeking Bilingual Specialization must also show evidence of the following:

- Informs families about resources (such as physicians or community clinics) which provide services to families in their primary language

- Helps parents identify resources in their homes, families, and community that will support the development of both languages

c) Recommends activities families can do at home that support their child's development

Examples

- Helps families find ways to play and learn with their toddlers (such as sending home activity bags, storybooks, manipulatives, art materials, etc.)

- Shares ideas with parents about the learning opportunities for children in everyday household tasks and routines

- Suggests experiences and inexpensive/common materials that can support play and learning at home

Competency Standard V:

To ensure a well-run, purposeful program that is responsive to participant needs

Functional Area 12: Program Management

Candidate is a manager who uses all available resources to ensure an effective program operation. Candidate is a competent organizer, record keeper, communicator and cooperative co-worker.

Item 12.1 Candidate observes, documents and assesses each child's developmental/educational progress.

Indicator:

a) **Objectively observes and records information about children's behaviors and learning**

   Examples

   - Regularly observes each child's developmental/educational progress

   - When observing/documenting, only records behavioral facts (objective statements) rather than assumptions or subjective biases that could lead to misinterpretations (such as "Vincent smiled" rather than "Vincent was happy" or "Liana threw a block which knocked over Brandy's block castle" rather than "Liana wanted to knock over Brandy's block castle")

   - Collects observational examples to support concerns regarding potential learning or behavioral needs or abilities

b) **Analyzes and assesses multiple sources of evidence in order to set appropriate developmental goals for each child/group, planning curriculum accordingly**

Examples

- Uses multiple sources of evidence when assessing the strengths, interests, abilities, and needs of each child (such as written observations, information from parents, data from formal and informal observation tools, individual portfolios, work samples, etc.)

- Considers the cultural expectations of each child when interpreting observations and setting goals

- Reflects on previous experiences in order to make intentional choices when planning curricula

- Uses Individual Family Service Plans (IFSPs)to inform planning for children, when applicable

- Accesses resources such as state early learning guidelines, when available, as a guide for planning

 Candidates seeking Bilingual Specialization must also show evidence of the following:

- Makes use of available evaluation instruments in the second language

12.2 Candidate adheres to regulatory requirements and program policies.

a) Adheres to current local child care regulations and program policies

Examples

- Abides by all legal and program requirements

- Adheres to group size requirements

- Complies with teacher-child ratio requirements

- Can articulate the philosophy, goals and objectives of the program to others

b) Adheres to professional Mandated Reporting requirements related to abuse and neglect

Examples

- Recognizes symptoms of possible abuse and neglect

- Is alert to play or behavior that indicates physical or sexual abuse

- Seeks out resources for information and support if physical, emotional or sexual abuse is suspected, following state law in response

- Responds sensitively to child's and family's needs, collaborating in carrying out treatment plans

c) Maintains current records on children's health, safety and behavior

Examples

- Keeps up-to-date records (such as attendance, accident/incident reports, child health and emergency forms, etc.) as required by regulations or policies, sharing the information with parents, specialists and other center personnel, only when appropriate

- Retains parents' written authorizations of all persons allowed to pick up children from the program

12.3 Candidate maintains effective professional relationships.

a) Establishes cooperative interpersonal relationships with coworkers, colleagues, volunteers and supervisors

Examples

- Supports other staff by offering assistance and support when needed

- Works as a member of a team with others in the classroom and the program, including substitutes, parents and volunteers

- Coordinates program plans with parents, specialists and program personnel, when appropriate

- Maintains professional relationship with supervisors

- Accepts supervision in the performance of duties

- Participates in peer evaluation and is able to accept comments and criticism from colleagues, supervisors and parents in a constructive way

Functional Area 13: Professionalism

Candidate makes decisions based on knowledge of research-based early childhood practices, promotes high-quality in child care services and takes advantage of opportunities to improve knowledge and competence, both for personal and professional growth and for the benefit of children and families.

Item 13.1 Candidate commits to highest standards for professional practices.

Indicator:

a) **Protects the confidentiality of information about children, their families and the child care program**

Examples

- Discusses sensitive issues with discretion, only with appropriate staff, following up on their resolution

- Observes strict confidentiality regarding the private issues of children and families, except as required by laws for reporting child abuse and neglect

- Informs parents of confidentiality policy

b) **Conducts her/himself in a professional manner at all times**

Examples

- Demonstrates a clear understanding of job expectations

- Has a positive attitude and work ethic, maintaining energy and enthusiasm

- Arrives at work on time every day

- Dresses appropriately for the responsibilities of the position

- Displays good judgment when making decisions that affect the children in her/his care

13.2 Candidate works with other professionals and families to communicate the needs of children and families to decision makers.

a) Advocates for the needs of children and families

Examples

- Advocates for additional resources for individual children or some aspect of the program

- Promotes high quality services for children and families

- Stands for the rights of children and families in public forums

 Candidates seeking Bilingual Specialization must also show evidence of the following:

- Promotes the effective functioning of the bilingual program by attempting to clarify issues relating to bilingualism and multiculturalism

- Advocates for the needs of children and families who speak a different language and operate in a different cultural context

13.3 Candidate takes advantage of opportunities to continue professional growth.

a) Learns about new laws and regulations affecting child care, children, and families

Examples

- Keeps informed about child care practices, research, legislation and other developments in the field of early care and learning using a variety of methods, including online opportunities and digital media

- Keeps abreast of proposed regulatory, legislative and workforce issues that affect the welfare of young children and families

- Seeks information about laws/policies and support strategies for children and families child affected by physical/sexual abuse and neglect

b) Takes opportunities for professional and personal development by reflecting, joining professional organizations and attending meetings, training courses and conferences

Examples

- Is a "life-long learner," continuing to gain knowledge about child development and early childhood best practices

- Continues to increase knowledge about child development in order to help children and parents deal with typical developmental issues (such as separation anxiety, crying, dependency, willfulness, challenging behaviors, shyness, sexual identity and making friends)

- Regularly reflects on own performance to identify needs for professional growth

- Maintains an active membership in an early childhood association(s)

- Seeks information relevant to the needs of the children in her/his care from professional resources (such as journals, community college courses, workshops, online websites/trainings, etc.)

- Participates in Professional Learning Communities with colleagues and community members

- Seeks feedback from a trusted mentor or coach

- Increases knowledge about dual language learning and inclusion by reading, attending workshops and consulting professionals

 Candidates seeking Bilingual Specialization must also show evidence of the following:

- Stays informed about the latest developments in bilingual education by reading articles, attending workshops and consulting with professionals

- Maintains and works to increase fluency in her/his second language

Note:

Also included in the CDA Comprehensive Scoring Instrument at the back of this book, as an indicator of her/his professionalism, is **Item 13.4**, the Candidate's completion of the required Professional Portfolio during the CDA credentialing process.

Part 3

Additional Information & Resources

- Overseas Assessments
- ADA Accommodations
- Principles for Dual Language Learners
- CDA Professional Development Specialist Eligibility Requirements
- The CDA Verification Visit™ Reflective Dialogue
- CDA Exam Question Examples
- Glossary
- Application
- Forms
- Comprehensive Scoring Instrument

Overseas Assessments

The Council currently conducts CDA assessments only in the United States, Puerto Rico and in the overseas installations of the U.S. Military Child Development Services of all Military Branches. If Candidates outside the United States or Puerto Rico want to obtain the CDA Credential, they must contact the Council to discuss any special protocols and additional expenses.

ADA Accommodations

The Council for Professional Recognition's mission is to provide the opportunity for all early childhood education professionals to participate in a fair and standardized CDA assessment process to demonstrate their competence and knowledge.

The CDA credentialing process is in full compliance with ADA requirements. The Council will provide reasonable accommodations to all eligible Candidates who provide the proper medical documentation.

For more information, please contact the Council *before you apply* at 800-424-4310 to discuss any special arrangements that may need to be made for your CDA Verification Visit™ and CDA Exam.

Principles for Dual Language Learners

Young children whose home language is not English are participants in many early childhood centers and family child care homes. These children are referred to as dual language learners because they are either learning two languages simultaneously or adding a new (second) language to their primary (home) language. The following developmental principles and accompanying practice examples are presented separately to emphasize that they apply to all Competency Standards and Functional Areas. These principles and examples provide important guidance to help teachers work competently with dual language learners.

Developmental Context

Infants and toddlers exposed to two languages at home or in an early childhood program have the opportunity to develop basic language ability in two languages simultaneously (simultaneous dual-language acquisition). However, when young children (aged 3, 4 and 5 years) whose families' primary language is not English begin participating in a preschool or family child care home, they have most likely established basic language ability in their home language. For these children this opportunity for second language acquisition is referred to as sequential dual-language acquisition. Early childhood programs can also offer opportunities for second language acquisition to children whose home language is English. However, the following developmental principles and examples focus on young English language learners in preschool programs.

The research literature on second language acquisition identifies the following four developmental stages (Tabors, 2008; Espinosa, 2010):

1. Home language use

Young children who have established basic oral communication ability in their home language naturally enter the preschool setting using their familiar home language. The degree to which these children experience being understood by others depends on whether any of the adults or children speak their home language.

2. Nonverbal/observational period

When young children speaking their home language are frequently not understood, they begin speaking less and turn their attention to observing, listening and using and nonverbal means of communication. This developmental stage is very important as the child is actively learning the sounds, words, and rules of the new language. These children are building their receptive understanding of their new language — connecting the sounds and words to people, objects, and experiences. There can be wide variance in the amount of time any child operates at this stage of development.

3. Telegraphic and formulaic speech

Children begin trying out their new language, using simple words or phrases to express thoughts, requests, and directions. Although the child may not know the specific meaning of these words and phrases, dual language learners are focused on results — do they work for social interactions or achieve the desired response from an adult. This form of early language production also enables these children to begin participating in group singing or reciting rhymes.

4. Productive language

Dual language learners begin building their own original sentences using words and phrases they have been hearing and practicing. This is a gradual phase as children test what works and experiment with applying grammar rules of their new language. Each child's productive language is closely related to their expansion of receptive language.

Adults who successfully work with young dual language learners understand that although each of the above developmental stages build on each other, beginning to use productive language does not replace earlier phases in particular situations. In some circumstances a child will revert to nonverbal observation and listening. Effective teachers are also sensitive to numerous factors that influence the rate and proficiency of each child's acquisition of a new language — amount and quality of exposure to English; age and culture; motivation and interest in new language; personality; and degree of accepting relationships that support trying new language (Tabors, 2008). Understanding that there will be individual differences between children is essential to providing the best possible support for dual language development.

An extremely important component of good early childhood programs and family child care homes is providing a learning environment that is supportive of the language development of all children. For dual language learners this means providing age appropriate, individually appropriate, and culturally appropriate experiences that help children begin to understand and use the English language while simultaneously developing their primary (home) language. This includes encouraging parents to provide their children with a strong foundation in their home language.

When a child's second language (typically English) is used predominantly by the surrounding society, home language development and maintenance may become more difficult. Nevertheless, research shows that second language learners do best in school when they have a strong grounding in their home language (Espinosa, 2010; Oiler & Eilers, 2002; Slavin & Cheung, 2005).The loss of the first language can be detrimental not only for personal, familial, religious, and cultural reasons, but it can also negatively impact children's progress in school. Teachers can help families value and support their child to continue developing the home language while also learning a second language.

Indicators of Competence with Dual Language Learners

a) The competent Candidate working with dual language learners is knowledgeable about and respectful of child's family, culture, and home language.

Examples

- Seeks information about language spoken at home and child's proficiency in the home language.

- Expresses interest in, and respects, families' priorities related to their child including attitude toward maintaining home language and acquiring English.

- Makes effort to learn about child's home culture and beliefs as well as the people, pets, activities and objects that are familiar and important to the child. Incorporates appropriate artifacts and pictures into the center to help introduce English words and phrases for things already familiar to the preschooler.

- Maintains communication with families and/or child's primary caregiver to track the child's developmental gains in the home language.

- Is knowledgeable about and respectful of child's family.

- Asks parents for a few words in the home language that can be used to welcome the child in the classroom *(e.g., with parents' permission makes a tape recording of these words to use in the classroom to comfort their child and to help other children hear the sounds of the child's home language)*.

b) The competent Candidate working with dual language learners establishes responsive and accepting relationships to help children feel confident to engage in receptive and verbal communication in either language — home language or new language.

Examples

- Builds positive, warm, nurturing relationships with dual language learners so that they feel safe and less anxious. Speaks English in ways that help dual language learners understand: uses simple sentences, repeats what is said, uses gestures and facial expressions, points to objects, uses everyday vocabulary.

- Speaks English clearly and slowly but not loudly, simplifying language when needed as you would for a younger child who is just learning their first language so the child more easily hears and learns individual words and phrases.

- Uses repetition so child hears the same word or phrase multiple times and consistently paired with the same object, person, or action.

- Gradually complicates own language so dual language learners continue to make progress in vocabulary development.

- Individualizes interactions that help each child gain trust in new people and environment.

- Is responsive and encouraging when child attempts verbal communication in either language — home language or new language.

- Provides verbal respectful response in the language the child is attempting to speak *(if possible)*.

- Recognizes when child mouths words or says words to self and encourages these attempts.

- Provides social support for dual language learners — regular contact with other children or adults who speak their language to help support their identity and help them make sense of what's going on.

- Provides lots of time and opportunities for children to play and talk among themselves.

- Encourages interactions between dual-language learners and English-speaking children by modeling initiations *(e.g., Candidate says to a child "Ask Lili, may I play with you?").*

- Pairs an English language learner with an outgoing English-speaking child for certain periods during the day, so that the English-speaking child may help to integrate the English language learner into classroom activities.

c) **The competent Candidate working with dual language learners provides numerous appropriate experiences to help children gain receptive understanding of the new language — specifically, to hear the sounds of the new language and connect them to people, objects and experiences.**

Examples

- Uses predictable, comfortable classroom routines so dual language learners know what to expect and uses consistent language when referring to activities *(clean up time)* and objects *(cubby, house area, block area, monkey bars, etc.)* throughout the day in the classroom and outdoors.

- Provides pictures to accompany the daily schedule, classroom rules, and other print in the classroom to help children know the expectations even though they may not yet understand the language.

- Consistently accompanies verbal communications with gestures, actions, visual aids, or directed gaze to help child interpret directions *(e.g. models washing hands while saying "Let's wash your hands")* or descriptions of actions *(e.g. "Here is your jacket, or book, or snack")*.

- Helps children link English vocabulary to firsthand experiences with pictures, concrete objects and real-life events. For the most part, talks about the here and now, until children become more proficient in English.

- Selects books, songs and poems with repetitive language and repeats them frequently. Uses music and physical actions to help children learn new phrases and sentences *("Head, shoulders, knees, and toes")*.

- Reads books, if possible in child's primary language prior to reading the book in English, always pointing to pictures associated with words and phrases.

- Provides small group reading times using concept books or predictable texts *(like Brown Bear, Brown Bear)* with simplified vocabulary where children can clearly see the pictures and follow along. Reads the same book repeatedly, as long as children are enjoying it, to build comprehension. Reads *(or provides audiotapes)* in the child's home language.

- Describes in simple words and phrases the actions of the child *(e.g., "You are rolling the ball")* or actions of other children he/she is observing *(e.g., "Molly is rocking the doll")*.

- Places words at the end of the sentence to give emphasis to those words *(e.g. "You have red shoes. Billy has black shoes")*.

- Keeps alert to a dual language learner's use of non-verbal communication, such as pointing silently to a milk carton. Supplies the words in English for what the child is trying to convey *(e.g., "would you like more milk? Sure, I will be glad to give you more milk.")*

- Intentionally introduces new vocabulary words and uses the words throughout the day.

d) **The competent Candidate working with dual language learners provides experiences to encourage and help children practice sounds and words of the new language taking into account the stages and patterns of home language and English acquisition as well as information about each child's progress in cognitive, social-emotional, and physical development.**

Examples

- Encourages child to repeat words as she or he demonstrates what objects or pictures they refer to.

- Gives child lots of time to think about what they want to say and waits to offer options of the word or phrase they are searching for when the child appears to wish for help.

- Asks young learners of the second language close-ended questions and offers some options for their response *(e.g., "Do you want the doll or do you want the clown?").*

- Pauses and lets the child fill in the next word when reading books.

- Provides opportunities to be able to answer in chorus with all the children.

- Helps children go from non-verbal responses to more expressive responses *(e.g., child looks at his shirt with spilled juice and looks at the Candidate; Candidate responds "Do you need me to change your shirt?" Child: "change shirt." Candidate: "That is right, I will be glad to change your shirt.")*

- Is able to expand child's vocabulary *(e.g., child says "yucky." Candidate responds "Yes, the floor is really dirty, yucky").*

- Notices words or phrases the child says *("me", "like", "more")* and helps child build from those words or phrases *(Candidate says "I like you!" "You want more").*

- Provides experiences for the child to play with the sounds: lullabies, repetitive singing and games, poems that repeat words.

- Understands that code switching or language mixing are typical and natural aspects of second language acquisition and enhances communication, and does not impose rigid rules about language *(e.g., child says "me asustado del doggie." Candidate responds: "Oh, I know — you are afraid of dogs").*

- Models correct English version of a phrase used by a dual language learner *(e.g., if a child says "I goed to park," the Candidate responds: "You went to the park? Who went with you?")*

- Engages child in conversations of topics that are interesting and important to him/her and that are part of their life experience

- Provides English language learners opportunities for one-on-one interaction with another child or adult where they may be more comfortable trying out English. But also plans for English language learners to have small group experiences — sometimes with children who are English language learners and other times with mixed groups of English speaking and English language learning children because each context offers different growth opportunities.

- Helps children acquire skills, knowledge, and attitudes such as book knowledge and appreciation, print awareness, letter knowledge, and phonological awareness in their home language. Once acquired, these skills will transfer as children become proficient in English.

- Includes environmental print *(signs, labels, books, magazines, newspapers and other text)* in English and the child's home language.

References:

Espinosa, L. (2010). *Getting it right for young children from diverse backgrounds: Applying research to improve practice.* Upper Saddle River, NJ: Pearson.

Oller, K. D., & Eilers, R. E. (Eds.). (2002). *Language and literacy in bilingual children.* New York: Multi-Lingual Matters.

Slavin, R. E., & Cheung, A. (2005). A synthesis of research on language of reading instruction for English language learners. *Review of Educational Research,* 75 (2), 247-281.

Tabors, P.O. (2008). *One child, two languages: A guide for early childhood educators of children learning English as a second language (2nd ed.).* Baltimore: Paul H. Brookes Publishing, Co.

CDA Professional Development Specialist Eligibility Requirements

To conduct CDA Verification Visits™ as a CDA Professional Development Specialist, an individual must meet the following criteria:

Technology

- Must have a valid email address

- Must have access to the Internet

Personal

- Must be able to relate to people of various racial, ethnic, and socio-economic backgrounds

- Must be knowledgeable about local, state, and national requirements and standards for child care programs serving children aged birth through 5 years

- Must be able to conduct CDA Verification Visits™ during normal operating hours of early childhood programs

- PD Specialists conducting bilingual CDA Verification Visits™ must be bilingual

- PD Specialists conducting monolingual CDA Verification Visits™ must speak the language of the Monolingual Specialization

Education

- Must hold a Baccalaureate or Associate degree from an accredited college or university in one of the following disciplines:

  - Early Childhood Education/Child Development

  - Elementary Education/Early Childhood Education

  - Home Economics/Child Development

- The degree must include, at minimum, 18 semester or 24 quarter hours of coursework in Early Childhood Education/Child Development, focused on children birth through 5 years

Experience

Option 1:

For those with a Baccalaureate degree or higher, two years in a child care setting serving children from birth to 5 years of age to include:

- One year working directly with children as a caregiver, teacher, child life worker, social worker, or similar role and one year facilitating the professional growth of at least one other adult

Option 2:

For those with an Associate degree, four years in a child care setting serving children from birth to 5 years of age, to include:

- Two years working directly with children as a caregiver, teacher, child life worker, social worker, or similar role and two years facilitating the professional growth of at least one other adult

Note: Any early care and learning professionals who only partially meet the eligibility requirements, may still apply to become a Professional Development Specialist. A space is provided on the online PD Specialist application, in which interested parties will have the opportunity to provide further explanations. Final determinations of eligibility will be made by the Council.

The CDA Verification Visit™ Reflective Dialogue

The CDA Verification Visit™ concludes with a 45-50 minute Reflective Dialogue between Candidate and PD Specialist. The purpose of the Dialogue is to support the Candidate's growing skills of professional reflection and goal-setting. The agenda of the Dialogue is as follows:

Welcome, Clarifications (up to 10 min.)

Welcome

- The Professional Development (PD) Specialist begins by welcoming the Candidate and reviewing the agenda, expectations and goals for the session by saying "We will be spending 45-50 minutes together. My role is to assist you as you reflect on your continuing professional growth and set new goals for yourself."

Clarifications (optional)

- The PD Specialist uses this time to ask questions regarding any Items in the Comprehensive Scoring Instrument that may still need clarification after the Review and Observation. (i.e., "I wasn't able to read or observe anything about Nap Time. How do you make sure that it is 'a pleasant rest time for all children'?" or "I wasn't able to read or observe anything about how you facilitate meal times. Tell me about how you 'facilitate appropriate mealtime experiences'.")

Reflective Dialogue Introduction, Professional Philosophy Statement (10 min.)

Reflective Dialogue Introduction

- The PD Specialist introduces the Reflective Dialogue by explaining that:

    a. The reflective dialogue will not be scored.

    b. There are no "right" or "wrong" answers in the discussion we're about to have.

- The PD Specialist asks the Candidate to turn to the Reflective Dialogue Worksheet found on p. 143 in this book. During the Reflective Dialogue, she/he will use the Worksheet to record important points to remember about her/his Areas of Professional Strength and Areas for Future Professional Growth. She will then refer to her Worksheet, at the end of the Dialogue, as she/he sets goals and records possible steps to reach each goal.

Professional Philosophy Statement

- The PD Specialist and Candidate discuss the Candidate's Professional Philosophy Statement.

- The PD Specialist asks, "In what ways does your teaching practice reflect your professional philosophy?" or "That's really powerful. How do you make your philosophy come alive?"

Candidate Self-Reflection (10 min.)

Areas of Professional Strength

    a. PD Specialist: "What do you think/believe are your greatest areas of strength as an early childhood professional?"

    b. "Why? How did you develop these areas of strengths?"

    c. "How do you think your areas of strength may positively impact the children and families in your care?"

Areas for Future Professional Growth

    a. PD Specialist: "What do you think/believe are your greatest areas for future growth as an early childhood professional?"

    b. "Why do you think this area(s) is more challenging for you than the areas you mentioned as strengths?"

    c. "How do you think working on these areas for growth may positively impact the children and families in your care?"

PD Specialist Feedback (less than 10 min.)

One Area of Professional Strength

    a. PD Specialist: "Having reviewed your Portfolio and observed you working with children, here is the greatest area of professional strength I documented."

    b. "How did you develop this strength?"

    c. "How do you think this strength may positively impact the children and families in your care?"

One Area for Future Professional Growth

    a. "Here is an area for future professional growth that I documented."

    b. "How might growing in this area positively impact the children and families in your care?"

Goal-Setting & Action-Planning, Close (10 min.)

Goal-Setting

• PD Specialist: "Using the areas of strength and future growth that you've identified and written down on your Reflective Dialogue Worksheet, let's take some time to identify 1 – 3 professional development goals you might set for yourself." (Note: final goals are determined by the Candidate, never by the PD Specialist)

Action-Planning

• PD Specialist: "How will you achieve these goals and by when? Let's brainstorm some actions you might take and timelines for completion. Then you can write them in the appropriate spaces on your Worksheet."

• Candidate and PD Specialist both sign statements at bottom of Worksheet. (The Candidate commits to pursuing goals, the PD Specialist signs to witness the Candidate's commitment)

Close

• PD Specialist: "Thank you for spending this time in the Reflective Dialogue with me. I hope you found it valuable. The Council would like to encourage you to share your goals with a mentor or your supervisor – someone who might hold you accountable and support you in successfully achieving them as you continue to grow as an early childhood professional."

CDA Exam Questions

The following examples are provided as support for Candidates to understand the nature and structure of the questions they will encounter when they take the Exam. None of the example questions, below, are included in any form in the actual CDA Exam Candidates will take.

As you may notice, the CDA Exam has been carefully designed by national experts to focus on "real life" examples that illustrate a Candidate's ability to put early childhood theory, research and knowledge into practice with young children.

Functional Area: Safe

Which of the following foods is safest to give children old enough to eat solid foods but less than four years of age?

    A. Cut-up hot dogs

    B. Peanuts

    C. Whole grapes

    D. Fine-cubed pears

Answer: D. Fine-cubed pears are softer and more easily eaten than the other food choices given. A, B and C are more apt to cause choking.

Functional Area: Healthy

A program has six babies ranging from five to ten months old. All are on their own feeding schedules. What approach to feeding should the program have?

    A. Maintaining the feeding schedules the babies already have

    B. Creating a new four-hour schedule for feeding the babies

    C. Obtaining the parents' permission for a common schedule

    D. Using the schedule of the infant with the best weight

Answer: A. An infant's health is best served when the caregiver maintains the feeding schedule that the infant has at home. B, C, and D would impose a schedule based on some other consideration than the infant's own cues.

Functional Area: Cognitive

One-year-old Jasmine repeatedly puts blocks in a pail and then dumps them out. How should Jasmine's teacher respond?

    A. By suggesting a more creative use of the blocks

    B. By telling Jasmine that the pail should be used for sand or water

    C. By encouraging Jasmine to continue, expanding her interest in the concepts of "empty" and "full"

    D. By prompting Jasmine to begin a different kind of activity

Answer: C. Jasmine's teacher should build upon her interest in filling and emptying the pail. A and B suggest that something is faulty about what she is doing and D ignores her discovery.

Functional Area: Communication

What is the best way to promote language development in infants under one year old?

    A. Talking to them about their environment and singing to them

    B. Hanging mobiles that are made of alphabet letters over their crib

    C. Allowing toddlers and older children to play with the infants

    D. Keeping recorded songs and a television set on throughout the day

Answer: A. Infants learn through the interactions that Choice A describes. B can be unsafe and does not contribute to an infant's language development. C requires monitoring and cannot be relied on as a means of language development in the program setting. D is not interactive.

Functional Area: Self

Which teacher practice is the most effective for helping build toddlers' sense of self-worth?

    A. Taking time to listen to and interact with each child

    B. Making sure all the children receive the same kind of praise

    C. Displaying the pictures and objects that the children produce

    D. Giving rewards often to children who work and play well

Answer: A. Relating to children as individuals fosters their sense of self-worth. B does not show regard for individual differences. C is a good thing to do but has limited ongoing value for building self-worth if done without A. D encourages children to focus on the reward and therefore may prove counter-productive for building self-worth.

Functional Area: Program Management

What is the primary purpose of making observational notes on individual children?

    A. To gain useful factual information concerning the child

    B. To describe the child's progress in a favorable light

    C. To verify that the program is doing what it claims to be doing

    D. To provide support for judgments the teacher has made

Answer: A. Observational notes should provide objective statements concerning a child's behaviors. B, C, and D promote the use of subjective judgments.

Glossary of Terms

The following glossary has been arranged in the general order of the CDA Credentialing Process and of this Competency Standards book; the order in which a Candidate might encounter each term.

General

Bilingual Program
A Bilingual program is one which has specific goals for achieving bilingual development in children, in which two languages are consistently used in daily activities and in which families are helped to understand the goals and to support children's bilingual development.

Candidate
An individual who has applied for and has met all eligibility requirements for the CDA Credential.

CDA
The Child Development Associate® Credential.

Competence/Competency
Skill or ability to do something well.

Competency Standards
Criteria that define the skills that a competent early care and learning professional should demonstrate in working with young children. There are six CDA Competency Standards, 13 Functional Areas, as well as Items, Indicators and Examples that provide further illustrations of the concepts presented. The six Competency Standards are:

    I.   To establish and maintain a safe, healthy learning environment

    II.   To advance physical and intellectual competence

    III.   To support social and emotional development and to provide positive guidance

    IV.   To establish positive and productive relationships with families

    V.   To ensure a well-run, purposeful program responsive to participant needs

    VI.   To maintain a commitment to professionalism

The term Competency Standards is also often used as a shortened name for this book.

Developmental Context

The CDA Competency Standards include a Developmental Context for each of the 13 Functional Areas. It includes a brief summary of children's development and a context for a caregiver's work with children at different stages of development.

Dual Language Learners

Children who are learning two languages simultaneously or adding a new (second) language to their primary (home) language.

Functional Area

A category of responsibility that defines a caregiver's role in relation to children. The six CDA Competency Standards are sorted into the thirteen Functional Areas: Safe, Healthy, Learning Environment, Physical, Cognitive, Communication, Creative, Self, Social, Guidance, Families, Program Management, and Professionalism.

Language Specialization

Candidates may choose to add Specializations to their CDA Credential

- Bilingual Specialization (for Candidates working in bilingual programs)

- Monolingual Specialization (for Candidates working in programs in which a language other than English is spoken)

① Prepare

Clock Hour

60 minutes. Used to determine the 120 required hours of professional education.

Family Questionnaires

The Candidate distributes a Family Questionnaire to each family that has a child in her/his group. The questionnaires give families an opportunity to describe/evaluate the Candidate's work from their point of view and give feedback to the Candidate.

Professional Education

Child care training/preparation for work with children and families. A Candidate must have completed 120 clock hours of such preparation. The CDA Candidate must have had comprehensive instruction in early childhood education/child development in the eight CDA Subject Areas.

Professional Portfolio

The collection of documentation of the Candidate's ability to meet all CDA eligibility requirements. The Portfolio also provides the compilation of the Candidate's reflections on how her/his practice meets the CDA Competency Standards. The Portfolio consists of:

- Transcripts/certificates/letters; documentation of the Candidate's professional education

- Family Questionnaires

- Six Reflective Statements of Competence

- The Resource Collection

- The Professional Philosophy Statement

Application

The online form that you will use to notify the Council that you are ready for your assessment (the CDA Verification Visit™ and the CDA Exam). If you are unable to use the online application, you may use the paper version found at the back of this book on p. 129.

Candidate ID Number (#)

The number assigned to you by the Council for Professional Recognition. The number appears in your Confirmation Note and on the printout you receive at the test center confirming that you completed the CDA Exam.

CDA Professional Development (PD) Specialist

The early childhood education professional, trained and endorsed by the Council to conduct your CDA Verification Visit™.

Conflict of Interest

A relationship that may interfere with an Professional Development (PD) Specialist's ability to be objective in assessing a Candidate. Relationships with Candidates that are unacceptable for serving in the PD Specialist role:

- Immediate relative (mother, father, sibling, spouse, son, daughter)

- Current direct supervisor

- Co-worker in same group/classroom

Ready to Schedule Notice

The email or paper notice you will receive from the Council after your CDA application and assessment fee have been successfully processed. The notice allows you to schedule the CDA Exam and gives you the deadline to complete the CDA Exam.

The CDA Exam

Confirmation Note

The letter or email you receive from PearsonVUE that confirms your CDA Exam appointment.

Flag

If you are not sure of your answer to an exam question, you may "flag it" for later review by clicking the "flag" button on the computer screen. At the end, if time permits, you will have a chance to review the questions you flagged.

My Account

The account you will create through the PearsonVUE website through which you will schedule and keep track of your CDA Exam.

Nondisclosure Agreement

The required statement seen at the start of the CDA Exam in which you confirm that you are taking the exam because you wish to earn the CDA Credential.

Password

The secret word known only to you that you will use along with your username to enter My Account on the PearsonVUE website to schedule your CDA Exam.

PearsonVUE

Owner and provider of the test centers where you will take the CDA Exam.

Review Screen

The computer screen that will be presented to you after you click through all 65 CDA Exam questions. The screen will show you which questions you have answered (complete), which you have not answered (incomplete) and which questions you flagged for a later review. You may then choose to go back to the various exam questions, if time permits.

Rules Agreement

Agreement that outlines the rules you must follow at the test center. You will be asked to sign the Agreement before entering the testing room.

Username

The unique name you will create, along with your password, that you will use to enter My Account on the PearsonVUE website to schedule your CDA Exam.

Valid Photo ID

The form of identification you must present at the test center in order to take the CDA Exam. Any identification that has not expired and includes your photo will be acceptable. Please note: the name on the ID must match exactly the name you entered on your application.

The CDA Verification Visit™

Comprehensive Scoring Instrument (CSI)

The official form used by the Professional Development Specialist to ascertain and record the Recommended Scores of the Candidate in the 13 Functional Areas using the Candidate's Professional Portfolio and a direct observation of her/him working with children.

Recommended Scores

The Item-level scores determined by the PD Specialist using the Comprehensive Scoring Instrument. The PD Specialist will submit Recommended Scores online to the Council upon completion of the CDA Verification Visit™. These scores are considered "recommended" as they reflect the recommendation of the PD Specialist but do not, in any way, fully determine whether a CDA Credential will be awarded. The CDA Verification Visit™ Recommended Scores must be combined with the CDA Exam score in order to reach the Cumulative Score the Council will use to determine if the CDA Credential has been earned/awarded.

Reflective Dialogue

The conversation between the Candidate and PD Specialist at the conclusion of the CDA Verification Visit™ in which the Candidate reflects on her/his areas of strength and areas for professional growth for the purpose of setting professional goals. The Reflective Dialogue is not scored and therefore has no bearing on the award of the CDA Credential.

The R.O.R. Model™

"R.O.R." stands for Review-Observe-Reflect™, the model used to structure the tasks undertaken by the CDA Professional Development Specialist during the CDA Verification Visit™ that contribute to the assessment of Candidate competency. The PD Specialist will Review the Candidate's Professional Portfolio, Observe the Candidate working with children and Reflect with the Candidate on her/his professional strengths and opportunities for growth.

Credential

The written document from the Council for Professional Recognition that verifies that an early care and learning professional has met the CDA Competency Standards.

Renewal

The process of revalidating a CDA Credential when it expires. The CDA Credential is valid for three years from the date of award or renewal. You may apply for renewal of the Credential 90 days before it expires.

The Child Development Associate® (CDA) Credential™ Application

Instead of using this application, consider applying online for faster results!
To fill out this Application online please visit, www.cdacouncil.org/yourCDA.

Please print legibly and be sure to retain a photocopy for your records. Your CDA credentialing time will be significantly increased if your application is not legible. APPLICATIONS THAT ARE INCOMPLETE OR MISSING PAYMENT WILL BE RETURNED.

A. Candidate Information

First Name*: ☐☐☐☐☐☐☐☐☐☐☐☐☐☐☐   Middle Name: ☐☐☐☐☐☐☐☐☐☐

Last Name*: ☐☐☐☐☐☐☐☐☐☐☐☐☐☐☐☐☐☐☐☐☐☐☐☐☐

Mailing Address*: ☐☐☐☐☐☐☐☐☐☐☐☐☐☐☐☐☐☐☐☐☐☐☐☐☐

Address Continued: ☐☐☐☐☐☐☐☐☐☐☐☐☐☐☐☐☐☐☐☐☐☐☐☐☐

City*: ☐☐☐☐☐☐☐☐☐☐☐☐☐☐☐☐☐☐   State*: ☐☐   Zip Code*: ☐☐☐☐☐

Email: ☐☐☐☐☐☐☐☐☐☐☐☐☐☐☐☐☐☐☐☐☐☐☐☐☐

Primary Phone #*: ☐☐☐☐☐☐☐☐☐☐   Alternate Phone #: ☐☐☐☐☐☐☐☐☐☐

Last 4 digits of Social Security Number*: ☐☐☐☐   Date of Birth*: ☐☐ ☐☐ ☐☐☐☐
                                                              Month   Date   Year

* indicates required field

B. Credential Type

Setting (check only one):

☐ Infant/Toddler
   (Birth to 36 months)

☐ Preschool
   (3 to 5 years)

☐ Family Child Care
   (Birth to 5 years)

Language Specialization (optional):

☐ Monolingual Spanish

☐ Bilingual (English and Spanish - see p. 33)

☐ Other monolingual (please indicate other language) _____

☐ Other bilingual, English and (please indicate other language) _____

The Type of Program I am currently working in:

☐ Private Child Care   ☐ Head Start

☐ High School Vocational Program   ☐ Family Child Care

☐ Military Installation _____

☐ Other _____

C. CDA Exam

I will the take the CDA Exam in the following language (check only one):

☐ English ☐ Spanish

Special Accommodations (optional):

I require special accommodations for my CDA Exam. My special accommodations request has been reviewed and approved by the Council and I have attached the signed approval form given to me by the Council. Please see p. 108 for further details.

☐ No

☐ Yes   *If yes: please attach a written explanation and the required official documentation to this application.*

D. Payment

Application Fee: $425.00

Please note that the Application fee is non-refundable and non-transferable. Applications sent without payment will not be processed. Only check, money order or credit card payments will be accepted. Cash will not be accepted.

☐ Enclosed is a non-refundable check or money order made payable to the Council for Professional Recognition.

☐ An agency is paying all or part of my application fee. I have enclosed my payment authorization letter as a substitution for my payment.

☐ I would like to pay with a credit card. ☐ VISA ☐ MASTERCARD ☐ DISCOVER

Card Number: ☐☐☐☐ ☐☐☐☐ ☐☐☐☐ ☐☐☐☐   Dollar Amount: $_____

EXP Date: ☐☐☐☐   CVC Code: ☐☐☐
Month Year   (3-digit number from back of card)

Name on Card: _____

Billing Address: _____

City: _____ State: _____ Zip Code: _____

Authorized Signature: _____

E. Education

Note that proof of your education will be verified by your Professional Development Specialist during your CDA Verification Visit™. You will need to show valid transcripts, letters or certificates documenting completion of your education.

Please check that you have completed at least ten hours of education in each of the following eight subject areas.

I certify that I have completed a minimum of 10 hours of education related to:

☐ Planning a safe and healthy learning environment.

☐ Advancing children's physical and intellectual development.

☐ Supporting children's social and emotional development.

☐ Building productive relationships with families.

☐ Managing an effective program.

☐ Maintaining a commitment to professionalism.

☐ Observing and recording children's behavior.

☐ Understanding principles of child development and learning.

Total education hours:

☐ I certify that I have completed at least 120 total clock hours of professional ECE education.

Required:

☐ All of my education meets Council requirements as outlined on pp. 10-11.

☐ None of my eligible education was obtained at conferences or from individual consultants.

☐ I have included transcripts, certificates or official letters documenting my education in my Professional Portfolio. I understand that my Professional Development Specialist will review them during my CDA Verification Visit™.

F. Eligibility Requirements

☐ I have a minimum of high school diploma / GED or I am enrolled in a high school career/ technical program in early childhood education/child development.

☐ I am able to speak, read and write in the language of my assessment well enough to fulfill the responsibilities of a CDA-credentialed professional.

☐ I have my current certificate of completion or card from a) any first aid course and b) an infant/child (pediatric) CPR course.

☐ I have distributed and collected my Family Questionnaires within the past six months.

☐ The Number of Family Questionnaires distributed and collected: _____

☐ I have 480 hours of experience within the past three (3) years working with children in the same age group and setting for which I am applying.

☐ I have completed my Professional Portfolio within the last six months and according to Council requirements.

My Professional Portfolio, includes:

☐ Majority of Family Questionnaires distributed were collected

☐ Six Reflective Competency Statements were written

☐ Portfolio includes all of the required Resource Collection items

☐ One Professional Philosophy Statement was written

☐ *For Infant/Toddler Candidates only:* met all additional requirements

☐ I understand that individuals convicted of a crime involving child abuse or neglect are ineligible to apply for or hold the CDA Credential. If I am awarded the CDA Credential, I agree to meet the standards of the CDA to the best of my ability. I also agree to conduct myself in a professional manner and abide by the *NAEYC Code of Ethical Conduct.* I testify that all answers given to all questions on this application are true to the best of my knowledge.

Candidate Signature: _____   Date: _____

G. My CDA Professional Development (PD) Specialist

In order to complete the CDA credentialing process, Candidates must participate in a CDA Verification Visit™ during which their Professional Portfolios will be reviewed, they will be observed working with children and they will participate in a reflective dialogue with a CDA Professional Development (PD) Specialist. Applications will only be accepted that include a confirmed PD Specialist for each Candidate (please see p. 20 for information on finding your PD Specialist). Once you contact your PD Specialist and confirm their willingness and availability to serve in this role, ask them to provide you with their full name and PD Specialist identification number:

Full Name of PD Specialist: _____

PD Specialist ID #: _____

NOTE: For those applying for a bilingual or monolingual credential, you must also confirm that the PD Specialist listed above is proficient in the language(s) to be used in the CDA Verification Visit™.

☐ I hereby confirm that I have been in direct contact with the person listed above and that she/he has agreed to serve as my PD Specialist. If I have checked this box falsely I am aware that I may be ineligible to receive the CDA Credential and my application fee will not be refunded.

H. Optional Demographic Data

Individual data provided below is optional and will not be shared. The aggregate data will be used for the Council's research purposes only. Your name will remain confidential.

Gender: ☐ Male ☐ Female

Race/Ethnicity:
☐ African American ☐ Asian
☐ Hispanic ☐ Native American
☐ White ☐ Other: _____

Primary Language: _____

Second Language (if applicable): _____

Highest level of education achieved:
☐ High School ☐ Two year college
☐ Four year college ☐ Graduate degree

CDA professional /in-service education (check all that apply):
☐ Four-year college ☐ Two-year college
☐ Career/Technical school ☐ Head Start
☐ Early childhood agency (non Head Start)
☐ Other: _____

If working with children, current title:
☐ Education supervisor / coordinator / specialist
☐ Assistant teacher / Aide ☐ Classroom teacher
☐ Program/Center Director ☐ Home Visitor
☐ Family Child Care Provider ☐ Student
☐ Other: _____

I. Director's Permission Statement (to be filled out by Director, please print legibly)

Full Name: _____

Email address: _____

Center or Family Child Care Program

Center/Program Name: _____

Center/Program Phone #: _____ Director Phone #: _____

Is your center or program licensed or meet state requirements?
☐ Yes ☐ No

If no, is the center or program exempt from licensing?
☐ Yes ☐ No

NOTE: *CDA Verification Visits™ cannot take place at centers that are not licensed or meet state requirements.*

Director Statement

I understand that a CDA Professional Development (PD) Specialist will conduct a CDA Verification Visit™ at my center/in my program. The CDA Verification Visit™ will include a review of the Candidate's portfolio, a classroom observation, and a reflective dialogue.

☐ I agree to find a quiet space for the PD Specialist to spend one hour reviewing the Candidate's portfolio, should the PD Specialist request this space.

☐ I understand that the observation will last for two hours and must take place while the Candidate is actively leading children's activities.

☐ If the Candidate needs to participate in the required reflective dialogue during the work day, I understand that I will need to provide a private space and 45-50 minutes of time during which the Candidate will be away from her/his group of children.

I verify that I am the Director or Family Child Care Provider identified or named in this form. All information I have provided here is accurate. I commit to respect the confidentiality of the Candidate as she/he moves through the CDA credentialing process.

Signature: _____ Date: _____

MY CDA Professional Portfolio

_____   _____
Candidate Name   Candidate ID Number

Use the following checklist to organize your Professional Portfolio in the order listed below. You may check off each item in the last column as it is completed. Use this "My CDA Professional Portfolio" sheet as the cover sheet inside your Portfolio. Please see pp. 12-20 for a detailed explanation.

TAB	REQUIRED PORTFOLIO ITEM		✓
	"My CDA Professional Portfolio" cover sheet (this document)		
A	**"Summary of My CDA Education"** cover sheet followed by all relevant training transcripts, certificates and official documentation		
B	**"Family Questionnaires"** cover sheet followed by all completed, returned Family Questionnaires		
C	**Reflective Competency Statement I**	CS I, including paragraphs CS I a, CS I b, CS I c	
C	**CS I Resource Collection Items**	RC I-1, RC I-2, RC I-3	
D	**Reflective Competency Statement II**	CS II, including paragraphs CS II a, CS II b, CS II c, CS II d	
D	**CS II Resource Collection**	RC II-1 through RC II-9	
E	**Reflective Competency Statement III**	CS III, including paragraphs CS III a, CS III b	
E	**CS III Resource Collection**	RC III	
F	**Reflective Competency Statement IV**	CS IV, including paragraphs CS IV a, CS IV b, CS IV c	
F	**CS IV Resource Collection Items**	RC IV-1 through RC IV-4	
G	**Reflective Competency Statement V**	CS V, including paragraph CS V a	
G	**CS V Resource Collection Items**	RC V	
H	**Reflective Competency Statement VI**	CS VI, including paragraphs CS VI a, CS VI b	
H	**CS VI Resource Collection Items**	RC VI-1, RC VI-2, RC VI-3	
I	**Professional Philosophy Statement**		

I attest that the following Professional Portfolio includes Resource Collection items that I gathered, myself, as well as original Statements written by me that reflect my work with the children and families in my care.

_____   _____
Candidate Signature   Date

Summary of My CDA Education

_____

Candidate Name

Note to Candidate: Please use this summary document as the cover sheet to your "education documentation"; the collection of transcripts, letters, certificates, etc. that you will place in your Professional Portfolio to document how you met the educational requirements for the CDA Credential. At your CDA Verification Visit™, your CDA Professional Development Specialist will review this sheet to ensure that it accurately reflects your education documentation that follows. Please see p. 11 for a detailed explanation of acceptable professional education.

Statements of CDA Education Completion:

I attest to completing the required 10 hours of education in each of the following CDA Subject Areas.

CDA Subject Areas	Please initial below
1. Planning a safe, healthy learning environment	
2. Advancing children's physical and intellectual development	
3. Supporting children's social and emotional development	
4. Building productive relationships with families	
5. Managing an effective program	
6. Maintaining a commitment to professionalism	
7. Observing and recording children's behavior	
8. Understanding principles of child development and learning	

I attest to the accuracy of the above Statements of Completion: that I completed at least 10 clock hours of professional education in each of the 8 CDA Subject Areas. I also attest that I have met or exceeded 120 total clock hours of CDA-related professional education.

_____   _____
Candidate Signature   Date

Family Questionnaire

Introduction

_____ is preparing to earn the nationally-renowned Child Development Associate® (CDA) Credential™. In order to be awarded the CDA, she/he has taken on a significant professional challenge: She/he must have experience working with young children, must have a required amount of early childhood education, must prepare a Professional Portfolio, must be observed working by a skilled professional (a CDA Professional Development Specialist) and must pass the national CDA Exam.

The process of getting a CDA is also a professional development experience in which Candidates reflect on areas of strength and areas for future professional growth. In addition to self-reflection, Candidates are provided feedback to consider by the CDA Professional Development Specialist and by you, if you so choose. So, we invite you to complete the questionnaire, below, in order to provide feedback that may help the Candidate continue to grow as a professional.

Please know that:

a) Completing this questionnaire is optional. If you choose to complete it, your feedback will only be read by the Candidate in order to contribute important information that may assist her/him in setting professional goals for the coming year. **The answers you provide on this questionnaire will have no impact on whether the Candidate will be awarded the CDA Credential.**

b) You may provide your feedback anonymously, if you so choose.

If you choose to complete the questionnaire, you must return it to the Candidate by _____.

Family Questionnaire

Each of the following topics relates to key areas of quality early childhood professional practice as outlined by the Council for Professional Recognition. For each area, please rate the Candidate on a scale of 1 – 3 in which 1 = Needs improvement/Area for professional growth, 2 = Capable/Competent and 3 = Very capable/Area of strength.

The Candidate:

1. Provides a safe, clean environment for my child and teaches her/him how to stay safe

1	2	3

2. Provides an environment that promotes health and good nutrition

1	2	3

3. Provides activities, materials and schedules that promote my child's development and education

1	2	3

4. Uses activities, materials and equipment that allow my child to develop small muscle skills (like writing or pouring) and large muscle skills (like climbing or balancing)

1	2	3

5. Uses activities, materials and equipment that help my child learn how to think, reason and solve problems

1	2	3

6. Helps my child learn how to communicate and introduces her/him to the basics of reading and writing

1	2	3

7. Helps my child express herself/himself creatively through music, art and movement

1	2	3

8. Nurtures my child, helping her/him build a positive self-identity and respect for every child's cultural backgrounds

1	2	3

9. Helps my child learn how to socialize and get along with others

1	2	3

10. Uses effective strategies to help my child understand how to behave appropriately

1	2	3

11. Establishes positive, responsive and cooperative relationships with myself and the members of our family

1	2	3

12. Is well-organized and effectively manages the classroom or group

1	2	3

13. Presents herself/himself in a professional manner

1	2	3

14. (for Bilingual Specialization Candidates only) Respectfully communicates with my family in our preferred language

1	2	3

_____

Name (optional)

Thank you for taking the time to support the Candidate's professional growth. If you would like to provide additional feedback, please feel free to attach it to this questionnaire.

COUNCIL
— for —
PROFESSIONAL
RECOGNITION

Cuestionario para la Familia

Introducción

_____ se está preparando para obtener la nacionalmente reconocida credencial de Asociado en Desarrollo Infantil (CDA). Con el fin de recibir esta credencial CDA, él/ella ha tomado un desafío profesional significativo: Él/ella debe tener experiencia trabajando con niños pequeños, debe tener una cantidad de cursos requeridos de educación infantil, debe preparar un Portafolio Profesional, debe ser observado(a) por un profesional calificado (un Especialista CDA en Desarrollo Profesional) mientras trabaja con niños y debe aprobar el Examen CDA.

El proceso para obtener la credencial CDA también es una experiencia de desarrollo profesional en la que el Candidato reflexiona sobre sus áreas de fortaleza y sus áreas para un futuro desarrollo profesional. Además de la auto-reflexión, a los Candidatos se les brinda comentarios sobre su desempeño que deben considerar. Estos comentarios los ofrece el Especialista CDA en Desarrollo Profesional y usted, si usted decide colaborar. Por ello, le invitamos a completar el cuestionario que se encuentra abajo, con el fin de brindar comentarios que puedan ayudar al Candidato a continuar su desarrollo como profesional.

Por favor, sepa que:

a) Completar este cuestionario es opcional. Si usted decide completarlo, sus comentarios solo serán leídos por el Candidato con el fin de proporcionar información importante que pueda ayudarlo(a) a establecer sus metas profesionales para el próximo año. **Las respuestas que usted brinde en este cuestionario no tendrán impacto en la decisión de otorgar o no la Credencial CDA al Candidato.**

b) Usted puede brindar sus comentarios de manera anónima, si lo desea.

Si usted elige completar el cuestionario, debe devolverlo al Candidato antes del _____.

Cuestionario para la Familia

Cada uno de los siguientes temas se relaciona a las áreas claves de prácticas profesionales de calidad en educación infantil indicadas por el Concilio para el Reconocimiento Profesional. Para cada área, por favor califique al Candidato en una escala de 1 – 3 en la cual: 1 = Necesita mejorar/Área para el desarrollo profesional, 2 = Capaz/Competente y 3 = Muy capaz/Área de fortaleza.

El Candidato:

1. Brinda un ambiente seguro y limpio para mi hijo y le enseña cómo permanecer seguro.

1	2	3

2. Brinda un ambiente que fomenta la salud y la buena nutrición.

1	2	3

3. Brinda actividades, materiales y horarios que fomentan el desarrollo y la educación de mi hijo.

1	2	3

4. Utiliza actividades, materiales y equipo que permiten a mi hijo desarrollar las habilidades de su motricidad fina (como escribir o verter líquidos) y las habilidades de su motricidad gruesa (como trepar o balancearse).

1	2	3

5. Utiliza actividades, materiales y equipo que ayudan a mi hijo a aprender cómo pensar, razonar y resolver problemas.

1	2	3

6. Ayuda a mi hijo a aprender cómo comunicarse y le presenta los conceptos básicos de lectura y escritura.

1	2	3

7. Ayuda a mi hijo a expresarse de manera creativa a través de la música, arte y movimiento.

1	2	3

8. Brinda afecto a mi hijo, ayudándolo a edificar una identidad positiva de sí mismo y respetar los orígenes culturales de cada niño.

1	2	3

9. Ayuda a mi hijo a aprender a cómo socializar y llevarse bien con otras personas.

1	2	3

10. Utiliza estrategias eficaces para ayudar a mi hijo a comprender cómo comportarse de manera apropiada.

1	2	3

11. Establece relaciones positivas, receptivas y cooperativas conmigo y los miembros de nuestra familia.

1	2	3

12. Es bien organizado y dirige eficazmente el salón de clases o grupo.

1	2	3

13. Se comporta de una manera profesional.

1	2	3

14. (sólo para Candidatos de Especialización Bilingüe) Se comunica respetuosamente con mi familia en nuestro idioma de preferencia.

1	2	3

_____

Nombre (opcional)

Gracias por tomarse tiempo para apoyar el crecimiento profesional del Candidato. Si le gustaría brindar comentarios adicionales, por favor no dude en adjuntarlos a este cuestionario.

COUNCIL
— for —
PROFESSIONAL
RECOGNITION

Family Questionnaires Summary Sheet

_____   _____
Candidate Name   Candidate ID Number

Once you have distributed and collected your Family Questionnaires, place them behind Tab B in your Professional Portfolio. Complete this Summary Sheet and put it in front of the completed questionnaires.

1. I distributed _____ Family Questionnaires.

2. I collected _____ Family Questionnaires and placed them behind this Summary sheet. Therefore, I collected the "majority" (more than half) of the Questionnaires I distributed.

3. I have looked for patterns or trends of feedback from these Questionnaires. Upon reflection, I think some of the families see the following as my greatest professional strength(s) and area(s) for professional growth:

Area(s) of Strength (list at least one)

_____

_____

_____

Area(s) for Professional Growth (list at least one)

_____

_____

_____

4. I have taken the areas of strength and growth that I wrote, above, and entered them into Boxes A and B in my Reflective Dialogue Worksheet at the end of this book.

Note to the PD Specialist:

Please do not read the contents of the Family Questionnaires found behind this Summary Sheet. This feedback is private, between this Candidate and the families she/he serves. Simply count the Questionnaires and verify that the number of questionnaires behind this Summary sheet matches the number written in #2, above. If the number matches, consider this required task complete. If the number does not match record this information in Item 13.4 of the _Comprehensive Scoring Instrument_.

CDA Verification Visit™ Reflective Dialogue Worksheet

Note to Candidate: The last step of the CDA Verification Visit™ process is the Reflective Dialogue, the culminating activity designed to support your ongoing reflection about your professional practices. Please know that the dialogue you will have with your CDA Professional Development (PD) Specialist will be kept confidential between the two of you, will not be scored and has no bearing on the award of your CDA Credential. You will retain this Worksheet after the dialogue – no one else will see this worksheet unless you choose to share it. Therefore, feel free to reflect honestly and candidly about your professional strengths and areas for growth. There are no "right" or "wrong" answers in a reflective dialogue – only your commitment to your own professional growth and the goals you will set for yourself.

Step 1: Identify Areas of Strength and Areas for Future Professional Growth

In order to identify the best goals for yourself, it may be helpful to first explore different perspectives – (1) opinions from the families you serve, (2) your own thoughts and (3) feedback from your CDA PD Specialist, who has just read your Professional Portfolio and observed you working with children. Before your CDA Verification Visit™, please read the Family Questionnaires you received. Look for trends or patterns of responses and write down, in boxes A and B below, as many areas of strength and areas for professional growth that you would like. You will complete the second and third columns during the Reflective Dialogue.

	1. Family Questionnaires (to be completed by the Candidate prior to the CDA Verification Visit™)	2. Candidate Self-Reflection (to be completed by the Candidate during the Reflective Dialogue)	3. Feedback From My PD Specialist (to be completed by the Candidate during the Reflective Dialogue)
What are Your Area(s) of Professional Strength?	A	C	E
What are your Area(s) for Future Professional Growth?	B	D	F

Step 2: Set Goals, Plan Action Steps

Now that you have listed your perceived strengths and areas for future growth, what goal or goals might you set for yourself? Is there a strength you're committed to strengthening even further? Is there an area you've identified that you are committed to improving? In the spaces below, list up to three professional goals you are committed to achieving. After writing each goal, discuss with your PD Specialist steps you might take to reach that goal.

Goal #1:	Steps I could take to reach Goal #1:
Goal #2:	Steps I could take to reach Goal #2:
Goal #3:	Steps I could take to reach Goal #3:

Step 3: Commit to Achieving Your Goal(s)

I, _____, hereby commit to achieving my goal(s) in order to further develop as a **professional and to become even more effective at serving the needs of the children and families in my care.**

_____   _____
CDA Candidate (sign here)   as witnessed by my CDA PD Specialist (sign here)

This worksheet is now yours to keep. Being a reflective practitioner and meeting the goals you've set for yourself is up to you, regardless of whether you are awarded your CDA Credential. The Council encourages you to share your goals with a mentor, colleague or supervisor who will support you, hold you accountable for meeting your goals and celebrate with you when you have met them.

COUNCIL —for—
PROFESSIONAL RECOGNITION

Comprehensive Scoring Instrument

Candidate's Name: _____

Credential Type: ☐ Infant/Toddler   ☐ Preschool   ☐ Family Child Care

Bilingual Specialization: ☐ Yes ☐ No

Date of Portfolio Review: _____

Date of Observation: _____

Instructions for the CDA Professional Development (PD) Specialist:

The CDA Comprehensive Scoring Instrument (CSI) is the tool you will utilize to determine the competencies of the Candidate named above, using multiple sources of evidence:

    (1) the contents of the Candidate's Professional Portfolio

    (2) your direct observation of the Candidate working with young children and

    (3) your skilled perceptions of the care/education environments that the Candidate is responsible for designing/maintaining (when applicable)

Structure of the CSI

The CSI was designed to reflect the nationally-recognized CDA Competency Standards, found on p. 40. in this book, that provide a baseline of competencies for all professionals working with, educating and caring for groups of young children.

In order to best elaborate on the key professional practices identified, the Standards in this tool have been arranged according to the following hierarchy:

Functional Area

Item/Item/Item

Indicator

CDA PD Specialists are responsible for using the CSI tool to determine and submit to the Council Recommended Scores (1 – 3) at the Item level. In order to assist you in this endeavor, it is recommended that you review and observe at the Indicator level, later using your professional judgment to assign Item scores based on the averages or patterns you have recorded of that Item's related Indicators.

In order to best determine Indicator scores you may need to consult the various optional examples listed in the Competency Standards section of the book. Please remember that these examples are optional and are provided only for the purposes of illustration. They were not designed to be an inclusive list that every Candidate must display in order to be assigned a Recommended Score.

Please also note that the CSI has been designed as a universal tool that can be used for all CDA Credentials: Preschool, Infant/Toddler and Family Child Care. Indicators must be interpreted using the specific examples listed in the book related to that Credential type (in other words, preschool examples may be different than infant/toddler examples). Additional examples have also been provided and must be taken into consideration for certain Items when reviewing and observing a Candidate applying for Bilingual Specialization.

Leave these CSI pages attached to the book during the CDA Verification Visit™ in order to quickly consult the examples for clarification whenever needed.

Use of the CSI

You will rate the Candidate on a scale of 1 – 3:

1	2	3

   1 = Little or no evidence

   2 = Some evidence

   3 = Great deal of evidence

Full instructions for use of the CSI can be accessed by PD Specialists in the CDA Professional Development Specialist Resource Library. Note: When submitting a score of 1 to the Council online, the PD Specialist will be required to add a brief note explaining the rationale and/or examples for that score.

Sections of the CSI

In order to make your use of the tool as efficient as possible during the CDA Verification Visit™, the CSI has been sorted into three color-coded sections:

Settings & Activities

This section includes all of the Items that do not rely on Candidate behaviors. In other words, you will be able to assess these Items without the Candidate present; by reading the related topics in the Candidate's Professional Portfolio and/or by looking at the children's environments (spaces, furniture, equipment, materials, etc.) for which the Candidate is responsible.

NOTE: If the Candidate is not responsible for designing/maintaining the environment(s) in which the Observation occurs, you will need to rely more heavily on the related writings/resources found in her/his Reflective Competency Statement about Competency Standard I: Safe, Healthy Learning Environments when reviewing the Portfolio.

Actions & Interactions

This section will be the primary section used during your observation of the Candidate working with children (minimum of two hours). All of the Items in this section relate to Candidate behaviors; the ways you observe she/he acting and interacting with children.

Review

This section includes all of the Items that are typically unobservable. In order to determine Recommended Scores for each of these Items, you will likely need to rely solely on what you read in the Candidate's Professional Portfolio during the one-hour Review session.

Final Steps

The final step, once you have completed the Review and Observe sessions using this CSI, is to facilitate the Reflect Session with the Candidate. During this session, you may ask questions of clarification to assist you in completing the CSI. You will also discuss the Candidate's Professional Philosophy Statement and provide the Candidate with your feedback about one "Area of Professional Strength" and one "Area for Professional Growth" based on your review and observation. To prepare, feel free to use the "Reminders to Myself to Prepare for the Reflective Dialogue" sheet found on the last page of this CSI.

Upon completion of the CDA Verification Visit™, you must remove the CSI from this book using the perforations on the inside of each page. You will then return the book to the Candidate and take the CSI with you in order to use when you submit this Candidate's Recommended Scores to the Council through the Submission Tool in the online PD Specialist Portal.

In order to protect Candidate confidentiality, the PD Specialist may not share or make copies of the notes or Recommended Scores recorded on the CSI with/for any person, including the Candidate. Once the Recommended Scores have been submitted to the Council online, the PD Specialist is required to shred or otherwise destroy this CSI tool.

Functional Area 1: SAFE

Item 1.1 Environments are safe for all children and adults. (p. 43)

| 1 | 2 | 3 |

Indicator:

a) _____ Materials, equipment and environments are safe

Item 1.2 Well-planned and well-organized emergency procedures and supplies are evident. (p. 44)

| 1 | 2 | 3 |

Indicators:

a) _____ Procedures for fires and other emergencies are posted

b) _____ First-aid supplies and medicines are stored appropriately and accessible to adults only

Optional Notes: SAFE (Items 1.1, 1.2 above)

Review Notes	Observe Notes

Functional Area 2: HEALTHY

Item 2.1 Children's settings promote good health. (p. 46)

| 1 | 2 | 3 |

Indicators:

a) _____ Materials, equipment and environments are clean and promote good health

b) _____ Disinfecting and sanitizing solutions are present and stored appropriately

c) _____ Relevant health information from families of children are maintained and posted

Optional Notes: HEALTHY (Item 2.1 above)

Review Notes	Observe Notes

Settings & Activities

Functional Area 3: LEARNING ENVIRONMENT

Item 3.1 Environments are developmentally appropriate for young children. (p. 51)

| 1 | 2 | 3 |

Indicators:

a) _____ Environments are pleasant, welcoming and provide appropriate levels of stimulation

b) _____ Environments are arranged and organized intentionally to meet the developmental needs of children

Item 3.2 Developmentally appropriate materials are available. (p. 53)

| 1 | 2 | 3 |

Indicators:

a) _____ Materials are developmentally appropriate for all children

b) _____ A variety of materials are provided for children to explore

c) _____ There is a sufficient number of materials to accommodate the group size

d) _____ Materials are organized and accessible to children throughout the day

Item 3.3 Daily schedule and weekly plan(s) are developmentally appropriate. (p. 54)

| 1 | 2 | 3 |

Indicators:

a) _____ Schedule allows for routine needs of children to be met

b) _____ Schedule provided meets children's needs for play

c) _____ Whole group times, when offered, are developmentally appropriate

d) _____ Weekly Plans provide a variety of developmentally appropriate experiences

e) _____ Pleasant nap or quiet times meet children's needs for rest

Optional Notes: LEARNING ENVIRONMENT (Items 3.1, 3.2, 3.3 above)

Review Notes	Observe Notes

Settings & Activities

Functional Area 4: PHYSICAL

Item 4.1 Activities, materials and equipment encourage children of varying abilities to develop their large muscles. (p. 61)

1	2	3

Indicator:

a) _____ Gross motor skills are encouraged through developmentally appropriate materials, equipment and indoor/outdoor activities

Item 4.2 Activities and materials encourage children of varying abilities to develop their small muscles. (p. 61)

1	2	3

Indicator:

a) _____ Individual fine motor skills are encouraged through a variety of developmentally appropriate materials and activities

Item 4.3 Activities and materials encourage children to develop their senses. (p. 62)

1	2	3

Indicator:

a) _____ Sight, sound, smell, taste, and touch experiences are encouraged through a variety of developmentally appropriate materials and activities

Optional Notes: PHYSICAL (Items 4.1, 4.2, 4.3 above)

Review Notes	Observe Notes

Functional Area 5: COGNITIVE

Item 5.1 Activities encourage curiosity, exploration and discovery. (p. 64)

1	2	3

Indicator:

a) _____ Activities involve developmentally appropriate, hands-on experiences

Settings & Activities

Item 5.2 Materials and equipment stimulate children's thinking and problem solving. (p. 64)

1	2	3

Indicators:

a) _____ Materials and equipment provide a variety of opportunities for cognitive development

b) _____ Materials chosen are meaningful to the children

Optional Notes: COGNITIVE (Items 5.1, 5.2 above)

Review Notes	Observe Notes

Functional Area 6: COMMUNICATION

Item 6.1 Materials promote early literacy. (p. 67)

1	2	3

Indicators:

a) _____ Literature/storytelling/bookmaking materials are provided

b) _____ Developmentally appropriate books are available

Item 6.2 Activities promote language development. (p. 68)

1	2	3

Indicators:

a) _____ Children are read to every day

b) _____ Activities advance the development of language acquisition and writing skills

c) _____ Activities provide frequent opportunities for children to listen, talk and express their ideas effectively

d) _____ Activities support the needs of dual language learners (when applicable)

Optional Notes: COMMUNICATION (Items 6.1, 6.2 above)

Review Notes	Observe Notes

Settings & Activities

Functional Area 7: CREATIVE

Item 7.1 Activities and materials encourage children to express themselves through the visual arts. (p. 74)

1	2	3

Indicators:

a) _____ Art materials and activities are available for children daily

Item 7.2 Activities and materials encourage children to dance, move and develop their musical abilities. (p. 74)

1	2	3

Indicators:

a) _____ Music and dance/movement materials and activities are available for children daily

Item 7.3 Activities and materials provided encourage children to develop their imaginations. (p. 75)

1	2	3

Indicators:

a) _____ Dramatic play materials and activities are available for children daily

Optional Notes: CREATIVE (Items 7.1, 7.2, 7.3 above)

Review Notes	Observe Notes

Functional Area 8: SELF

Item 8.1 Children's environments support the development of positive self-concepts. (p. 79)

1	2	3

Indicators:

a) _____ Spaces and activities help each child develop a sense of self-identity/worth

b) _____ Materials chosen provide children opportunities to experience success

Settings & Activities

Optional Notes: SELF (Item 8.1 above)

Review Notes	Observe Notes

Functional Area 9: SOCIAL

Item 9.1 **The classroom environment provides opportunities for children to experience cooperation.** (p. 84)

| 1 | 2 | 3 |

Indicator:

a) _____ Materials, equipment and activities provided help children experience working and playing in harmony

Item 9.2 A non-biased environment is provided. (p. 84)

| 1 | 2 | 3 |

Indicator:

a) _____ Diverse activities, materials, curricula and/or events reflect multiple cultural groups, ethnicities and family structures

Optional Notes: SOCIAL (Items 9.1, 9.2 above)

Review Notes	Observe Notes

Settings & Activities

Functional Area 10: GUIDANCE

Item 10.1 Spaces and materials are arranged to promote positive interactions and limit disruptive behaviors. (p. 88)

1	2	3

Indicator:

a) _____ Spaces and materials provided anticipate children's behavioral and developmental needs

Optional Notes: GUIDANCE (Item 10.1 above)

Review Notes	Observe Notes

Functional Area 11: FAMILIES

Item 11.1 Various opportunities to appreciate and communicate with children's families are included as part of the regular program. (p. 94)

1	2	3

Indicators:

a) _____ Room displays and materials reflect respect for various communities, cultural groups and families

b) _____ Opportunities to communicate with and distribute information to families are provided

Optional Notes: FAMILIES (Item 11.1 above)

Review Notes	Observe Notes

Settings & Activities

Functional Area 1: SAFE

Item 1.3 Candidate ensures children's safety at all times. (p. 44)

1	2	3

Indicators:

a) _____ Ensures that children are attended by authorized adults at all times

b) _____ Teaches children appropriate safety practices

c) _____ Provides attentive supervision at all times

d) _____ Makes sure that foods that are known choking hazards are not served

Optional Notes: SAFE (Item 1.3 above)

Review Notes	Observe Notes

Functional Area 2: HEALTHY

Item 2.2 Candidate implements appropriate hygiene practices to minimize the spread of infectious diseases. (p. 46)

1	2	3

Indicators:

a) _____ Cleans/sanitizes materials and equipment

b) _____ Uses correct hand washing procedures before and after serving food, diapering/toileting and whenever needed

c) _____ Implements sanitary diapering/toileting procedures

Item 2.3 Candidate encourages children to practice healthy habits. (p. 48)

1	2	3

Indicators:

a) _____ Ensures that older children wash hands properly, with assistance when needed

b) _____ Models, communicates and provides activities that teach the importance of good health to children and families

Item 2.4 Candidate provides appropriate mealtime experiences. (p. 49)

| 1 | 2 | 3 |

Indicators:

a) _____ Serves nutritious meals and snacks

b) _____ Facilitates appropriate mealtime experiences

Optional Notes: HEALTHY (Items 2.3, 2.4, 2.5 above)

Review Notes	Observe Notes

Functional Area 3: LEARNING ENVIRONMENT

Item 3.4 Candidate's disposition is warm and welcoming. (p. 56)

| 1 | 2 | 3 |

Indicator:

a) _____ Creates a nurturing relationship with each child

Item 3.5 Candidate demonstrates sound judgment in using the posted Weekly Schedule/Daily Plan. (p. 57)

| 1 | 2 | 3 |

Indicators:

a) _____ Generally follows posted schedule and plan

b) _____ Veers from schedule and plan as needed

Item 3.6 Uses a variety of strategies to transition children from one activity to another. (p. 58)

| 1 | 2 | 3 |

Indicator:

a) _____ Demonstrates an understanding of the importance of transitions

Optional Notes: LEARNING ENVIRONMENT (Items 3.4, 3.5, 3.6 above)

Review Notes	Observe Notes

Actions & Interactions

Functional Area 4: PHYSICAL

Item 4.4 Candidate's facilitation promotes children's physical development. (p. 63)

1	2	3

Indicators:

a) _____ Participates in physical activities with children, when appropriate

b) _____ Guides the development of children's fine and gross motor skills

Optional Notes: PHYSICAL (Item 4.4 above)

Review Notes	Observe Notes

Functional Area 5: COGNITIVE

Item 5.3 Candidate's interactions promote children's thinking and problem solving. (p. 65)

1	2	3

Indicators:

a) _____ Facilitates children's thinking and creative problem-solving skills

Item 5.4 Candidate's interactions intentionally build upon children's previous knowledge. (p. 66)

1	2	3

Indicators:

a) _____ Connects concepts to children's prior experiences

b) _____ Supports children's repetition of the familiar

Optional Notes: COGNITIVE (Items 5.3, 5.4 above)

Review Notes	Observe Notes

Actions & Interactions

Functional Area 6: COMMUNICATION

Item 6.3 Candidate reads to children in a developmentally appropriate manner. (p. 70)

| 1 | 2 | 3 |

Indicators:

a) _____ Reads to children engagingly

Item 6.4 Candidate's interactions encourage children's communication skills. (p. 70)

| 1 | 2 | 3 |

Indicators:

a) _____ Promotes children's language development through her/his verbal and non-verbal communications

b) _____ Interacts with children, listening and responding appropriately

c) _____ Supports the needs of dual language learners (when applicable)

Item 6.5 Candidate promotes children's vocabulary development. (p. 72)

| 1 | 2 | 3 |

Indicators:

a) _____ Intentionally provides opportunities for children to learn new words.

b) _____ Regularly introduces children to more advanced vocabulary

Optional Notes: COMMUNICATION (Items 6.3, 6.4, 6.5 above)

Review Notes	Observe Notes

Functional Area 7: CREATIVE

Item 7.4 Candidate promotes individual expression and creativity. (p. 75)

| 1 | 2 | 3 |

Indicators:

a) _____ Encourages creative self-expression in children's activities

b) _____ Facilitates child-directed and process-oriented creative experiences

Actions & Interactions

Optional Notes: CREATIVE (Item 7.4 above)

Review Notes	Observe Notes

Functional Area 8: SELF

Item 8.2 Candidate's interactions help children develop positive self-concepts. (p. 80)

1	2	3

Indicators:

a) _____ Respects the individuality of each child

b) _____ Shows sensitivity to and acceptance of each child's feelings and needs

Item 8.3 Candidate encourages children to develop a sense of independence. (p. 82)

1	2	3

Indicators:

a) _____ Encourages children's self-help/self-regulation skills while being respectful of family preferences and cultural differences

b) _____ Ensures that toileting is a developmentally appropriate, positive experience for children

c) _____ Promotes each child's growing sense of autonomy

Optional Notes: SELF (Items 8.2, 8.3, 8.4 above)

Review Notes	Observe Notes

Functional Area 9: SOCIAL

Item 9.3 Candidate promotes children's sense of belonging in the classroom community. (p. 85)

1	2	3

Indicators:

a) _____ Encourages children's social interactions

b) _____ Models appropriate social interactions

Actions & Interactions

1 = Little or no evidence   2 = Some evidence   3 = Great deal of evidence

Item 9.4 **Candidate helps children experience sympathy/empathy and respect for others.** (p. 86)

1	2	3

Indicators:

a) _____ Helps children understand their feelings and the feelings of others

b) _____ Discusses diversity comfortably when interacting with children

Optional Notes: SOCIAL (Items 9.3, 9.4 above)

Review Notes	Observe Notes

Functional Area 10: GUIDANCE

Item 10.2 **Candidate proactively implements methods for preventing behavioral problems.** (p. 88)

1	2	3

Indicators:

a) _____ Acknowledges positive behaviors

b) _____ Models appropriate behaviors

c) _____ Provides firm, consistent limits and expectations

d) _____ Uses effective classroom management techniques

e) _____ Helps children learn to articulate their emotions and practice how to respond in challenging situations

Item 10.3 **Candidate uses positive techniques when reacting to children's challenging behaviors.** (p. 91)

1	2	3

Indicators:

a) _____ Places emphasis on the development of self-discipline/self-regulation

b) _____ Deals with challenging behavior in a consistent and calm manner

c) _____ Uses appropriate techniques to address negative behaviors

Optional Notes: GUIDANCE (Items 10.2, 10.3 above)

Review Notes	Observe Notes

Actions & Interactions

Note to the CDA Professional Development Specialist:

The following Items have been categorized as "Review" Items as they may not be fully observable in a typically-scheduled CDA Verification Visit™. Therefore the Council recommends that you primarily base your Recommended Scores on the Reflective Competency Statements and Resources in the Candidate's Professional Portfolio that you will read during the Review Session.

Functional Area 11: FAMILIES

Item 11.2 Candidate appreciates the uniqueness of each family. (p. 95)

1	2	3

Indicators:

a) _____ Welcomes and respects every family

Item 11.3 Candidate partners with families to support the needs of their children. (p. 94)

1	2	3

Indicators:

a) _____ Works closely with each family

b) _____ Maintains open communication with families

1	2	3

Item 11.4 Candidate helps families understand and support the healthy growth and development of their child. (p. 98)

Indicators:

a) _____ Provides information and opportunities to help families meet their child's developmental needs

b) _____ Knows the social service, health and education resources of the community, engaging them when appropriate

c) _____ Recommends activities families can do at home that support their child's development

Optional Notes: FAMILIES (Items 11.2, 11.3, 11.4 above)

Review Notes	Observe Notes

1 = Little or no evidence   2 = Some evidence   3 = Great deal of evidence

Functional Area 12: PROGRAM MANAGEMENT

Item 12.1 Candidate observes, documents and assesses each child's developmental/educational progress. (p. 101)

| 1 | 2 | 3 |

Indicators:

a) _____ Objectively observes and records information about children's behaviors and learning

b) _____ Analyzes and assesses multiple sources of evidence in order to set appropriate developmental goals for each child/group, planning curriculum accordingly

Item 12.2 Candidate adheres to regulatory requirements and program policies. (p. 102)

| 1 | 2 | 3 |

Indicators:

a) _____ Adheres to current local child care regulations and program policies

b) _____ Adheres to professional Mandated Reporting requirements related to abuse and neglect

c) _____ Maintains current records on children's health, safety and behavior

Item 12.3 Candidate maintains effective professional relationships. (p. 103)

| 1 | 2 | 3 |

Indicator:

a) _____ Establishes cooperative interpersonal relationships with coworkers, colleagues, volunteers and supervisors

Note: You may find some needed evidence for this Item during the Observe Session, if the Candidate is observed working with another teacher or colleague.

Optional Notes: PROGRAM MANAGEMENT (Items 12.1, 12.2, 12.3 above)

Review Notes	Observe Notes

Functional Area 13: PROFESSIONALISM

Item 13.1 Candidate commits to highest standards for professional practices. (p. 104)

1	2	3

Indicators:

a) _____ Protects the confidentiality of information about children, their families and the child care program

b) _____ Conducts her/himself in a professional manner at all times

Item 13.2 Candidate works with other professionals and families to communicate the needs of children and families to decision makers. (p. 105)

1	2	3

Indicators:

a) _____ Advocates for the needs of children and families

Item 13.3 Candidate takes advantage of opportunities to continue professional growth. (p. 105)

1	2	3

Indicator:

a) _____ Learns about new laws and regulations affecting child care, children, and families

b) _____ Takes opportunities for professional and personal development by reflecting, joining professional organizations and attending meetings, training courses and conferences

Reflective Competency Statements
were written

c) _____ Portfolio includes all of the required Resource Collection items

d) _____ One Professional Philosophy Statement was written

1 = Little or no evidence   2 = Some evidence   3 = Great deal of evidence   CSI 19

Review

Note to the CDA Professional Development Specialist:

One clear sign of the Candidate's professionalism is her/his completion of the Professional Portfolio as a requirement of the credentialing process. Therefore, the following Item should also receive a Recommended Score:

Item 13.4 Candidate has completed all requirements of the CDA Professional Portfolio in preparation for this CDA Verification Visit™. (pp. 12-20)

1	⊠	3

3 = All Portfolio requirements met

1 = One or more Portfolio requirements were not met

(If 1, the PD Specialist is required to add a brief note explaining the rationale and/or examples for that score)

Indicators:

a) _____ Majority of Family Questionnaires distributed were collected

b) _____ Six Reflective Competency Statements were written

c) _____ Portfolio includes all of the required Resource Collection items

d) _____ One Professional Philosophy Statement was written

Optional Notes: PROFESSIONALISM (Items 13.1, 13.2, 13.3, 13.4)

Review Notes	Observe Notes

Required Portfolio Components

If either of the following required Portfolio components do not meet requirements, you must notify the Candidate at the conclusion of the CDA Verification Visit™ that she/he will receive a postcard from the Council notifying her/him of the required procedures for correcting these errors within six months of her/his Ready to Schedule notice.

In the spaces below, write down the reason(s) the components do not meet requirements. You will then submit this information to the Council online, along with your Recommended Scores.

1. The Candidate's 120 clock hours of Professional Education meets all requirements (pp. 10-11):

☐ Yes   ☐ No

If "No," please explain: _____

_____

_____

2. The Candidate's First Aid/CPR certification meets all requirements (p. 14):

☐ Yes   ☐ No

If "No," please explain: _____

_____

_____

For the PD Specialist:

Reminders to Myself to Prepare for the Reflective Dialogue

Clarifications (complete this section after the Review and Observe sessions)

After reviewing this Candidate's portfolio and observing her/him working with children, I may still need to ask the Candidate some questions of clarification about the following topics that I was unable to read about or observe:

_____

_____

_____

_____

Professional Philosophy Statement (complete this section during the Review Session)

After reading the Candidate's Professional Philosophy Statement, here are one or more key topics about how she/he puts her professional philosophy into practice, that I may want to bring up as I facilitate the reflective dialogue:

_____

_____

_____

Professional Development Specialist Feedback (complete this section after the Review and Observe sessions)

After reading through this Candidate's Professional Portfolio and observing her/him working with children, I will mention the following Area of Strength and Area for Professional Growth during the reflective dialogue:

One Area of Strength

_____

_____

One Area for Professional Growth

_____

_____

Notes:

Notes: